The

Sensitive One

THE
SENSITIVE
ONE

a memoir

SUSAN FRANCES MORRIS

Published 2021
Printed in the United States of America
Print ISBN: 978-1-64742-161-8
E-ISBN: 978-1-64742-162-5
Library of Congress Control Number: 2021902733

For information, address:
She Writes Press
1569 Solano Ave #546
Berkeley, CA 94707

She Writes Press is a division of SparkPoint Studio, LLC.

Book design by Stacey Aaronson

To Bruce and my children—
Your love is everything to me

"This above all; to thine own self be true."

—WILLIAM SHAKESPEARE

THE BEGINNING

We all enter the world a blank slate. Free of thoughts and ideas. Who we eventually become is determined by the upbringing and experiences that fill that slate. We don't get to choose who will raise us. We don't control whether they'll be caring and loving, or distant and rejective.

If you were born lucky, home can be a pillar of strength. Supportive, safe, nurturing, and protective. A safety base from which we venture into the world. The root of our self-definition. A secure place to dream.

For those of us less fortunate, home can be a backdrop for pain. The place where growth is stunted. Where nurturing is nonexistent and dreams are slain. A place where love is replaced by apathy, compassion replaced by indifference.

THE DREAM

I could tell by the vibrant intertwined colors of red, blue, salmon, and scattered bits of green against a dark background that the flying carpet was the carefully handmade kind. An oriental one of Persian origin. Intricate woven patterns of tiny flowers and leaves along the border matched the multi-leaf pattern that adorned the middle. The beige fringe that dangled at either end is what I remember the most. It was this fringe that I'd clung to for many nights of my childhood.

The nightmare was a recurrent one. Every time, it began with the flying carpet floating through chilly air on a dismal day. I was nine, ten, eleven—always somewhere around there. My mom and grandmother sat cross-legged on the carpet toward the front, as if in the front seat of a car. I sat alone behind my grandmother, shivering. A vast dark ocean lay below. Suddenly, the wind would pick up and knock me around. I'd grab the beige fringe that hung off the edge and hold onto it for dear life. Terrified of the ocean below, I screamed, "Mom—help me—I'm falling!"

My grandmother, my mother's mother, to whom I was close, always exclaimed, adamantly, "Joan, Susan is falling off! If she falls, she's going to drown! You need to grab her!"

My mother's response was always the same: "I'm too busy driving this thing; I can't stop. If I stop now, we're *all* going to drown."

Screaming for help, I tumbled and spun toward the ocean's surface and slammed into the icy cold water. Then I began to sink to the bottom, still hoping my mother would save me. It was there on the dark ocean floor that my breathing slowed and became shallow. As I was about to take my last breath, I'd wake up—shaking and crying out.

As a child, I didn't know the meaning of the dream. I knew only that it was terrifying. There were many nights when I refused to go to sleep and begged my mom to stay with me in my bed. When I told her about the dream, she said, "Susan, that could never happen; try not to worry about it." But for years the nightmare returned.

I eventually stopped having that nightmare, but the memory of it has stayed with me. I think about it often. As an adult looking back on that horrid dream, I can see that it's a clear representation of my life.

Having courage
does not mean
that we are unafraid.

Having courage
and showing courage
mean we face our fears.

We are able to say,
"I have fallen,
but I will get up."

—MAYA ANGELOU

hat the heck was that? I silently asked myself. I was sitting in a meeting on patient safety with about twenty-five other nurses and doctors at Yale New Haven Hospital when out of the blue, I felt a pins-and-needles sensation in my right breast. *Why would I experience something that felt like a mini-letdown reflex at this point in my life*? I hadn't felt anything like this since breastfeeding my three children. For a moment, I smiled at the memory of them as babies: Sarah with her dark almond-shaped eyes and toothless smile grinning at me for the first time. Patrick who could be soothed only by being curled up in a snuggly attached to my chest. And, Samantha, who could sleep anywhere, playing in the snow. I would turn fifty-one next month; my youngest was thirteen years old, and I was pretty sure I was going through menopause. Though the pins-and-needles feeling was brief, it was enough for me to take pause. I looked away from the meeting and gazed out the wall of windows.

I WAS AN RN and worked at Yale New Haven Hospital as the manager of the postpartum units. Despite my nursing background, I knew very little about breasts other than teaching new mothers how to breastfeed. So, after the meeting was over, I sought out my friend Mary, a lactation consultant whose office was down the hall, to see if she had any insight into the sensation I'd felt in my breast. I figured it was just hormones, but I still wanted her opinion.

Mary was in her office working on her computer when I approached.

"Hey, Mary, do you have a second?"

Turning her chair around to face me, she replied, "Sure, Sue, what's up?"

"Well, I don't know, I just felt this tingling in one of my breasts, and I thought it was kinda weird." Cracking a smile, I said, "You're the breast expert, so I wondered if you'd ever heard of anything like that before. You know, maybe because of hormones in menopause."

"Not really," Mary said. "I haven't heard of anything like that, but you never know, right? Hormones do crazy things." Then her eyebrows crinkled as she asked, "How long did it last?"

"I don't know—five seconds or so."

"That *is* kinda weird. I can do a little research into it if you want.

I didn't want to waste her time over what was probably nothing. "No, that's all right, I said. "I just realized it's June, and I totally forgot my mammogram is due this month. I'll just make an appointment and mention it to them."

"All right. Well, let me know what happens."

After thanking her, I walked back to my desk, rested my hands on my forehead, and closed my eyes. My mind wandered back to my surprise fiftieth birthday party, almost a year earlier, and how that birthday had catapulted me into a new decade. I thought about all the changes I'd been through and what the next few months would bring. Because my husband Bruce had taken an 80-percent cut in pay when he entered the fellowship program, the one major change for me was that after working part time for the past thirteen years, I had gone back to work fulltime, not as a staff nurse but as a nursing manager to support our family while Bruce was working on his fellowship. I actually loved being the breadwinner for a change. And knowing that it would only be three years made it easier for me. The tables turned, Bruce had more time with Samantha, while I had less. He did all the things that I used to: bus pickup and drop off, soccer practice, making dinner, and countless other tasks that had filled my days.

The next few months would involve driving sixteen hours to our new home, in St. Louis Missouri, leaving my family and friends behind and doing all the things that entail setting up a new home

My thoughts returned to the tingling in my breast. It was really beginning to bug me. Was it something that I should be worried about? Does breast cancer have a feeling? I can't die at fifty. *Okay, Sue*, I said to myself, *you're making a mountain out of a mole hill. Don't wind yourself up.*

For the past three years, I'd been enjoying life in the winding back roads, rolling hills, and small-town feel of Farmington, Connecticut. Red barns, white fences that kept grazing horses from roaming, and fresh fruit stands became some of my favorite sights. After eleven years in East Longmeadow, Massachusetts, where Bruce had a private OB/GYN practice, we'd been ready for a change, so we moved to Farmington where Bruce had been accepted into the University of Connecticut's (UCONN) three-year fellowship program in maternal-fetal medicine (MFM). He'd always liked the challenge of high-risk pregnancy and was looking forward to the new direction.

Then three years were up. Bruce's fellowship was ending, and he accepted a position with an MFM group in St. Louis, Missouri. We'd be moving in less than a month, and although we were facing another big change, we were looking forward to a new chapter in our lives.

When I'd started dating Bruce seventeen years earlier, he was an OB/GYN resident in his second year of a four-year residency program, and I was a RN who worked on the labor and delivery floor of the same hospital. My feelings toward men at the time were murky at best. Since the explosive ending of my first marriage five years earlier,

I was happy living life as a single mom. My two children, Sarah and Patrick were ten and eight years old, and they were my life. A relationship seemed like a complication to me, and I didn't want any complications. But as Bruce and I continued to spend time together, my resistance weakened. He asked me out more and more, and being with him was a joy. On our first date, we went to see *The Nutcracker* at a small theatre in the town of Northampton, Massachusetts. After it was over, we walked to a quaint coffee shop all decked out in red and green, gold glitter, and a small Christmas tree adorned with mini white coffee ornaments. The steam from our hot drinks and the smell of gingerbread cookies floated through the air as we chatted. I loved the fact that Bruce looked directly into my eyes when I spoke; he made me feel special, which was an extremely unfamiliar sensation for me. Slowly the emotional barriers I had built up over so many years started to come down, and we became entangled in each other's lives.

In the fall of 1991, one year and ten months after we met, we married. Bruce and I talked about having more children. Two perhaps. I was thirty-five, so we started trying to get pregnant pretty quickly. It took two years for us to conceive, and Samantha was born when my older kids were fourteen and twelve. Sarah and Patrick welcomed their baby sister with open arms.

After Sarah, my first-born, arrived back in 1979, I'd suffered from the "baby blues." They hit me a few days after she was born. Sadness lingered, and crying came easily. When I looked at her with pride and awe, I wondered if my mother ever looked at me like that. The unconditional love I now felt was something I'd never experienced before, so why was I feeling so low? I read up about it and learned that having these blues was pretty common for new mothers, and that knowledge made me feel better. Then, before I knew it, the happiness I felt at being a new mom eclipsed the sadness. When Patrick was born two and a half years later, the blues ran deeper. This time the melancholy felt like someone had pulled a dark shade all the way down on my life. I realized that I couldn't remember the last time I'd smiled.

Three weeks after the cesarean section, I was still guarding my stomach and I had trouble picking up Sarah. When I did sleep, it wasn't much. At the end of April, the temperature spiked to 68 degrees, so I forced myself to go outside with Sarah and Patrick, hoping the fresh air would make me feel better. While I held Patrick in a snuggly against my chest, I pushed two-and-a-half-year-old Sarah on the aluminum swing set in our backyard. But I just couldn't bring myself to hoot and holler like I usually did when she went high on the swing. *What is the matter with me? I have these two beautiful children; I should be grateful and full of glee. Why do I feel so bleak?*

During my pregnancy with Patrick—the fighting in my marriage along with the emotional abuse escalated, and when I started to become intolerant of my husband's abusive ways, I became like a mother bear coming out of hibernation and fighting back to protect her cubs. He realized that I had changed, and he didn't like that. That April day, I understood clearly that I loved my children and despised my husband.

Knowing what I know now about postpartum depression, I realize that the signs and symptoms had been omnipresent—I just didn't recognize them. Now years later, I knew what to expect, but this time the depression didn't wait until after childbirth; it crept into my life during my pregnancy. The nurse in me knew that I might be living in emotional darkness for a while, and sure enough, I struggled with depression through Samantha's entire first year. Desperate for help, I started therapy with my previous therapist, Cindy, to deal with my constant anxiety and intermittent panic attacks. What I didn't know at the time was that the next six months would involve recovering repressed memories and nightmares and would at one-point employ hypnosis.

Two months after Samantha was born, I started to have random thoughts of cutting my baby, so for a time I became afraid of knives. Looking back on it now, I think her vulnerability frightened me. The rational part of my brain knew that I would never harm myself or my baby, but the irrational thoughts terrified me so much that I hid all the sharp knives and never told anyone about my thoughts. Not even my therapist. *If I tell Bruce or Cindy, they'll think I'm nuts and lock me up somewhere. They'll take my baby away.* So I suffered in silence and prayed daily for the thoughts to go away. I saw Cindy weekly, sometimes biweekly. We discussed anti-depressants, but I resisted taking them because I didn't want to stop breastfeeding. But the crazy thoughts didn't go away, so when Samantha was fourteen months old, I started taking an antidepressant.

Then, after months of not caring if the sun came out, I picked up my 35-mm camera, which I hadn't done in months and started taking pictures of my children. I looked forward to the day the photos would come back in the mail all developed. I started listening to my favorite music and sang along to the songs. And, to my delight, a few weeks after starting on the medication, I heard myself laughing again. That's when I knew I was on my way back. I was petrified of ever going through that darkness again, so Bruce and I agreed our family was complete.

THE TINGLING SENSATION I'd experienced in the meeting reminded me that I was due for my annual mammogram. As far as medical appointments go, I dreaded my yearly gynecological exam, and this was just as bad. My schedule was always jam-packed, so procrastination came easily. But I knew better than to ignore this strange symptom; my grandmother on my mother's side had had breast cancer. *Just get it done*, I thought.

Feeling some degree of relief from the decision to take a next step, I lifted my heavy head from my hands and looked out my office window at the beautiful view of the water on Long Island Sound. It brought me peace and clarity. Nature always did that for me. I picked up the phone and set up a mammogram appointment for the following week.

I sat in the mammography waiting room of the UCONN Medical Center feeling a roller coaster of emotions; my leg bounced up and down, and I picked at my fingernails. The mammography technician, Sherri, called my name and led me to the exam room. We chatted a little bit. She was the same person who'd done my mammogram the previous year, which I remembered because we'd talked about our teenage daughters. Although I hadn't seen her in a year, I remembered her fondly. I told her about the tingling feeling I'd experienced the week before in my right breast. She said, "Okay, then, let's do that side first."

Together, we walked over to a narrow, tall, rectangular X-ray machine that skimmed the ceiling. I stood facing the front of the machine and removed my hospital gown from my right arm. The technologist raised a black metal film holder, about the size of a placemat, to my breast level. She used her two hands to position my right breast on the cold plate, then guided my arm onto a grab handle. A plastic upper plate, called a paddle, was lowered and now my breast was held captive in between two compression plates. The pain was so intense, it stopped my breathing. On a scale of one to ten—an eleven.

"Make sure you keep your head turned away and hold your breath when I say to," Sherri instructed. And with that, she tightened the two plates, which compressed my breast into a pancake. The pain was intense but lasted only about five seconds. "Hold your breath," she said as she stood in front of a computer behind a protection window.

"Oh my," Sherri said. "This wasn't here last time, was it?" After she released the plates, I covered my right breast with the pink hospital gown. I felt a kinship to Sherri and asked her if I could take a look at it and then walked over to the digital screen. I'd never read mammogram films and I didn't know what I was looking for, but I was curious. As I stood dumbfounded, she pointed out the big fuzzy cotton ball on the otherwise blackish film. My prior mammogram films sat dormant to the side of the counter. Sherri picked up the one film from last year and held it up to the light, and then compared it to the one just taken. Looking at last year's films versus this year's, I could clearly see the difference. As I stood there staring at the screen, beads of sweat started to appear on my forehead and I could feel perspiration starting in my armpits. My hands went cold and a tingling feeling rose from my toes to my groin and up through my head. I was surprised that I was still standing, because I could have sworn, I'd dropped to my knees. I wanted to go home and crawl into bed. The white spot was right where I'd felt the tingling. *Where the hell did that come from and how long has it been there?* My breathing stopped.

I asked Sherri her opinion of what she was seeing, but like any medical professional, she didn't reveal much. Instead she tried to reassure me by saying that the radiologist was in today and would look at the results after we were finished taking films. Sherri took two more X-rays of the same breast at different angles. My mind whirled as we continued onto the left side, the entire time trying to figure out how to make this large dot disappear.

Fuck. The rationalizations began.

It has to be a lymph node or something.

Can cancer be that small?

Maybe it's fibrous tissue.

It has to be anything but the big C.

When Sherri was done with all the testing, she gathered up my chart along with my prior X-ray films, turned toward the door, and with a passing glance said, "I'll be right back. I'm going to have the radiologist look at this."

I sat silent in the exam room as the dark feeling of something-bad-is-about-to-happen started welling up inside me. It was the same feeling I'd had as a child when my dad came home drunk from work.

All of my past mammograms had been normal. I'd always gotten dressed, gone home, and forgotten all about it until about a week later when I'd receive a letter featuring that wonderful word "normal." Not today.

After about ten minutes, Sherri came back into the room and told me that they wanted to do some further testing right away. I was upset that the radiologist didn't come out of his office to tell me that himself.

"It is concerning," she said. "He wants you to have an ultrasound." So I was led out of the mammogram room and into the ultrasound waiting room. She'd told me it would take about fifteen minutes to get the room ready, so I asked if it was okay to go get my husband in another part of the building. The coin had flipped, and I was on the other side of the power dynamic. A patient. It wasn't at all like me to be passive, and it surprised me that I asked permission instead of telling them that I'd return shortly with my husband. I called Bruce, and he answered on the second ring. At my "Hello," he immediately knew something was wrong.

"Hey, Sue, Everything all right?"

"No," I paused. "Can I come down to your office?" I asked.

"Of course. I'm in the middle of something, but I'll meet you there," he said.

Trembling all over, I took the escalator down one flight and race-walked my way to Bruce's office.

"You look like you've just seen a ghost," he said.

"Something like a ghost, all right, if a ghost is big and round. It was definitely white."

After I told him about the mammogram and the big white dot, he tried to reassure me. "It's probably nothing." But I knew, just like I always do, that when Bruce is quiet, he's worried.

"Don't tell me it's probably nothing. My intuition tells me otherwise. I've never had any issues with my mammograms, and this dot *just happens* to be located exactly where I had that tingling feeling. I don't think this is just hormone related." I know how medical people act when they don't want to tell you something. I've given bad news many times. My God. This time I was the one waiting for the truth.

We hugged, and then silence took over.

Bruce took my hand in his and squeezed. He wrapped his index finger around my baby finger, the way we always held hands. I was overwhelmed by the comfort this gesture brought me. We walked down the long corridor back to the ultrasound waiting room and sat until my name was called.

Why is she so bubbly? I wondered after the nurse called my name. The ultrasound machine that would soon announce my fate was rolled to the foot of the table. It hummed in my ears like a car engine running quietly at idle. The radiologist, Dr. Zimmerman, walked in and introduced himself. He was short and pudgy with a round, clean-shaven face and black, wavy hair. His dark-chocolate-colored eyes matched his dark-rimmed glasses and had a sympathetic look to them. His crispy-clean, white lab coat with his name engraved above the pocket smelled of starch. He told us what he was going to do, and with Bruce by my side, I stared in silence at a stain on the white ceiling tile until he started the ultrasound. At that point my gaze shifted. I couldn't focus on anything but his expression. The lack of positive comments sent my mind into overdrive.

Everyone is so damn quiet.

What is everyone thinking?

Everybody is so serious.

The silence is killing me.

Somebody talk. Someone please say something.

Please, God, tell me this is not happening.

A glimmer of hope, a slight smile, anything—I'd take it. But he remained expressionless. Even the bubbly nurse's smile was gone. The doctor rotated the ultrasound screen toward us, so we could see the image on the screen. The dot looked much larger because it was magnified.

"It has micro-calcifications," he said.

What? What the heck is a micro-calcification, and what the fuck is it doing in my breast? I'm a nurse, I have a BS degree, I knew what *micro* meant, and that calcification had to do with how the body deposits calcium in the bones. But in my breast?

We watched as white dots appeared onto the screen. They looked like a troop of soldiers, all headed in the same direction, as if being pulled by some invisible magnetic force to join the one large white dot. I'd never seen an ultrasound this close up, and I wasn't really certain what I was seeing. But it sure didn't look good.

Oh shit, this cannot be good.

"What I am seeing is concerning," the doctor said. "This lump, or tumor as we call it, is about the size of a fingertip. I can't tell if it is benign or not. We need to do a biopsy to find out," he added.

There was no mention of cancer, but Bruce and I knew what the doctor was thinking. A doctor had just said "concerning."

I was advised to make an appointment for the following day to see a surgical oncologist. That's when I knew he expected it to be cancerous.

The next morning, Bruce and I were sitting in the waiting room of the oncologist's office, at the same hospital. I'd slept like crap, awakened anxious and cranky, and fought like crazy to keep my thoughts from going to the dark side. Bruce sipped coffee next to me.

We were pleasantly greeted by a nurse who introduced herself to me and asked how I was doing as Bruce and I were brought into an examination room. We were introduced to Dr. Ayer, and I liked her immediately. She sat with us and slowly reviewed the magnified version of the mammogram. Wow. The tiny dots didn't look so tiny anymore, and the large dot looked huge.

Dr. Ayer said, "Honestly, I'd be surprised if it wasn't cancer, based on what I'm seeing. Breast calcification is small calcium deposits that develop in a women's breast as they age. They're very common and usually benign," Dr. Ayer said. "But if the calcifications form a pattern or grow in tight clusters like these, they can be signs of cancer." My fear now had a name. Thoughts raced through my mind like dry leaves spiraling in the wind. Shit.

Am I going to die?

We discussed the next steps: I'd have the biopsy, she'd call me as soon as the results came back, and then we'll meet and go over the results together.

The timing couldn't have been worse. Our move to St. Louis was only one month away. We had a thousand details left to handle before being ready to relocate, and Bruce had just finished his fellowship. It was supposed to be a time of celebration. My staff had scheduled my going away party for the following day, and Bruce's celebration was the following evening.

We drove home, each deep in the silence of our own thoughts.

CHAPTER 2

1970–1972

When I was thirteen, my father's drinking took a sharp turn for the worse. While he used to return from his Friday night trip to the package store with a couple six packs of beer, now he came home with a case. He started waking us up in the middle of the night to look for tweezers, scissors, and combs, and for countless other nonsensical reasons. Because of this, I started to feel a deeper responsibility for my younger siblings. The two youngest were five years old and already followed me everywhere, and no one else seemed to notice that they were often left alone to fend for themselves. In effect, I functioned as the eldest sibling, even though, my sister Marie was two years older than I.

Mary and Margaret were the babies of the family, and my parents' second set of twins. My sister Sheila and I were the first set of twins, born eight years earlier. I'd always been close to my little sisters, and both held a special place in my heart from day one. I felt bad for them. I'd at least remembered my father when he'd been sober, but they'd have no memories of a dad who was happy, generous, or loving. The only father they'd ever known was drunk all the time.

I became the mother figure for Mary and Margaret. I didn't have to step up as I did, but my heart gravitated toward their sad eyes. I'd wake them up for school in the morning, read them bedtime stories, and tuck them in at night. Even though it wasn't true, I reassured them that although the house was in chaos, they were safe. They wrote me little notes with colorful hearts made with crayons, drawn with Xs and Os all over them. I'd find them tucked under my pillow at night, and on many nights, I hid similar notes for them. These notes filled my heart up. I'd leave them response notes on their pillows that they'd find when they woke up, and sometimes I'd hide the notes with clues on where to find them. The gleeful expressions on their faces when they'd find the notes were priceless. I loved seeing their smiles as they ran into my bedroom squealing, "Sue, I got your note!" There was nobody else in my life who made me feel like they had—useful, loved, and looked up to.

There were seven of us kids in all, products of an Irish Catholic marriage. Marie born in 1954; Susan and Sheila, 1956; Joan, 1958; Charles, 1961; Mary and Margaret, 1964. We'd eventually become known as "The McNally Girls." I don't think Charles liked that very much.

My mother was absent emotionally or physically during the chaos in our home caused by my drunken father. His benders occurred mostly on weekends when my mother worked as a nurse on the evening shift at the hospital. By dinner time, Dad was wobbly at best and would forget about us kids. Dinner became a can of Campbell's SpaghettiOs, or Chef Boyardee meat ravioli.

I took on the caretaking role. I was the one who got my younger siblings up and ready for school. Each weekday morning, I'd wake up to my blaring alarm, walk to the other side of my bedroom to shut it off, then lumber down the stairs. First stop, the bedroom that Joan and Charles shared. As always, I peeked in the door and said, "It's time to get up." If I didn't see any movement, I'd say it again, "It's time to get up guys. It's a school day." Then, back upstairs, to Mary and Margaret's room, which they shared with my oldest sister, Marie. Marie would be awake most mornings but not yet out of bed. Mary and Margaret always needed more nudging to rouse them. Last stop was back to my own bedroom to wake up Sheila, my twin and roommate.

In the afternoons and evenings, I would check Mary and Margaret's homework and read them bedtime stories, snuggle with them in bed until they fell asleep, and keep them as safe from harm as best I could. I had a hard time understanding why my mother wasn't capable of doing these things for her own children. And my mother also didn't have the energy to give me what I needed, which was attention and comfort. I never seemed to get any.

I didn't act out; I always followed the rules as a child. If the sign said, "Do not walk on the grass," I didn't even think about it. Because my mom acted as if the she had all the weight of the world on her shoulders, her daily irritability left me feeling that I was just in the way. The energy that my mom did have went to putting out the family's fires, like the broken brown glass bottles that smelled of beer or the broken dishes strewn about the kitchen on any given morning. Even though we were a family of nine, I grew up feeling alone and lonely.

The first time I intentionally harmed myself to get attention, I was around ten years old. I scraped my knee on purpose so that my bleeding leg would draw some affection from my mom. I did it only a few times and stopped because it never delivered my desired results: love, compassion, and perhaps even a hug. "You'll be fine, Susan," is what I heard over and over again as she put the band aid in place and sent me on my way.

The lack of love and security I felt in childhood set the stage for many years of my feeling unlovable. I continuously searched elsewhere for the feeling of security I was missing. The unhealthy choices I made along the way—harming myself, choosing abusive relationships, making bad social decisions—were the result of my attempts to hide my never-ending feelings of emptiness, loneliness, fear, and despair.

Over time I noticed a marked change in my father. Instead of going to work on Saturday mornings, he was now home. His beer drinking would start at lunchtime and end when he passed out some-time late in the evening. Mom became aloof, said, "Jesus, Mary, and Joseph!" a lot, and carried around her rosary beads always rubbing them. I absolutely craved a small token of my mother's love. I needed more than anything for her to tell me that everything was going to be okay, even if it wasn't. When I expressed a need, her response was always, "Susan, I just don't have it in me to give." I was on my own.

Just like the time I asked her if we could talk about something I was afraid of. I wanted to tell her that I was scared to be home with my dad when she was working. The week before I had sliced the bottom of my foot on something sharp in the backyard and it started gushing blood. I limped bleeding into the kitchen to find my dad taking another bottle of beer out of the refrigerator. He brought me to the bathroom; and as I cried, he tried to stop the bleeding—but he couldn't. He fumbled with the gauze pads and then dropped the entire box of band aids which went flying all over the tiled bathroom floor. I cried out, "I want Mom! You don't know what you're doing!" I tried to help him by putting pressure with a white washcloth, but bright-red blood continued to dribble onto the floor, and I was growing more and more frightened. All of a sudden, I stood up on one foot and demanded for him to bring me to our next-door neighbor Bettie's house. Bettie was like a sec-ond mother to all of us and always told us if we ever needed any-thing to come over.

Without much effort, Bettie got the piece of glass out with a pair of tweezers, stopped the bleeding, and bandaged me up. When my mom changed the bandage the next day she said; "You're lucky that you didn't need stitches, Susan, be careful next time." I sure didn't feel lucky. When I told my mom that I was afraid that next time something worse would happen and Bettie wouldn't be around, she told me I worried too much.

I often wonder if the recurring anxiety I'd later experience as an adult was an outcome of my mother never calming or reassuring me. I took it upon myself to tell my younger sisters what I myself wanted to hear. Even at that early age, I became aware of my own mothering instincts. They needed me, and it felt great to be needed.

When there was harmony in our family, I waited for turbulence. Frightening episodes didn't happen every day, but I felt like I was a passenger in a pilotless airplane. It was only going to be a matter of time before it crashed. Like the calm before a storm, a tranquil day or two in our house usually indicated that something bad was about to happen. And that something usually took the form of a raging alcoholic hurricane called "Dad."

IT WAS THE middle of the night when I was awakened by a high-pitched whistle followed by an insistent authoritative voice coming from the bottom of the stairs. It was the voice of my inebriated father. The shrill sound of the whistle blew again, and his voice got louder and closer. He flipped the switch to my overhead bedroom light, and my eyes blinked open.

Was there a fire or something? His bugged-out, bloodshot eyes sent a shiver down my spine. I cringed in fear, and was afraid I was going to pee my pants.

My father's breath sent the smell of beer and cigarettes into the room as he chanted:

"Up and at 'em!

"Rise and shine!

"Let's go downstairs.

"Everybody up, pronto.

"March!"

He stumbled over to my bed, abruptly pulled off my warm, yellow blanket, and threw it on the floor, exposing my bare, trembling, thirteen-year-old legs. Dazed and sleepy, I sat up and pulled the nightie over my wobbly knees, my eyes blinking from the bright light. *What's the matter with my dad? Did someone put a devil spell on him? Why is he screaming?*

Dad's half-lit cigarette dangled from his bottom lip, and I hoped the gray ashes wouldn't fall on me. I looked over at my twin sister, Sheila, in her bed. Her eyes were also wide open, both of us startled and speechless as he yanked the covers from her bed, too. He continued on into the bedroom across the hall to awaken Marie and the younger twins, who were five years old.

He barked:

"Time to get up!

"Let's go!

"Everybody downstairs.

"Time to put your thinking caps on!"

Although my dad had served a short term in the Air National Guard, he was not a military man. He was an attorney. But I imagined that this must have been what it was like to be an army soldier. He used words like "attention," "stand tall," and "march." We obeyed his, "March two, three, march two, three," down the stairs and into the kitchen, where he ordered us to sit single-file on the floor. Charles and Joan shared a downstairs room and were already sitting on the floor. Charles's frightened stare made me shiver as I took my place in line. We were powerless.

The seven of us sat sleepy-eyed on the kitchen floor, lined up in a straight row. As we did annually for Easter and Christmas photo shoots, we automatically lined up according to our ages. There we sat: Marie, age fifteen; Sheila and I, thirteen; Joan, eleven and a half; Charles, eight; and Mary and Margaret, only five years old. We were a clan. My back was straight against the eagle-printed wallpaper, and I was flanked by Marie and Sheila. A silver cross and gold-colored rotary phone hung above my head.

What's a thinking cap? I wondered. I looked down the row of my siblings, and every one of them looked terrified. I wondered if anyone else was also angry that our own father had woken us in the middle of the night like this. If they were, nobody said a word. They just kept their heads down.

"There are items missing from this house, and we need to find them. Now! Scissors, tweezers, and black combs!" my dad barked. The man with the silver whistle in his hand, screaming at us, looked like my father but was not acting like him. When he yelled like that, his face turned red, and sometimes spit flew out of his mouth.

The night before had been pretty uneventful. Mom, an RN, had been on the three-to-eleven second shift in the labor and delivery unit of the local hospital where she worked part time. Dad was responsible for cooking us dinner those nights. He had opened up his first bottle of beer while he cooked us hot dogs and beans for supper. I hated hot dogs and beans, especially the way he made them. He always burned the hot dogs, just like he burned bacon and eggs. We all ate on the picnic table in the backyard, each leaving the table after we finished. Then, my siblings and I watched TV until it was time for bed. Then, after we'd all gone to sleep, he had drunk more and became crazier and crazier.

"Where are the scissors, the black combs, and the goddamn tweezers? Why can't I find anything in this goddamn house?" he yelled louder. "How am I going to comb my hair in the morning?"

I didn't understand why my dad was obsessed with black combs, tweezers, and scissors. I thought all of these items naturally disappeared in a large family, kind of like white socks.

We whispered to each other, "Do you know where the combs are? Have you seen the tweezers anywhere?" We spread about the house barefoot, in our pajamas, pretending to search for the items. We took the sofa cushions off and looked all around and underneath the sofa. We searched the bathroom, the kitchen, and inside the trash basket. We pleaded with each other to find something so we could go back to sleep. My father had told me once when I'd lost something that I'd find it if I prayed to St. Anthony, the patron saint of lost things. So, I prayed, "Please, St. Anthony, let somebody find something so I can go back to my warm bed."

Well into our search, my mother emerged annoyed from her bedroom. "Bob, what do you think you're doing, waking the kids in the middle of the night?" she asked. "The kids need their sleep. Let them go back to bed." She told us all to go back to bed and said we could look for the items in the morning. I wondered what had taken her so long.

My father chanted the phrase, "Scissors—comb—tweezers" so many times that, after coming up empty-handed and being allowed to go back to bed, I still heard the chanting in my head. My bed was cold. I prayed again, "Please, God, let me sleep the rest of the night and not hear any more of my dad yelling." Mary and Margaret, still scared, tiptoed into my room and curled up next to me for the rest of the night.

THE NEXT MORNING, my dad handed me a twenty-dollar bill and said, "Susan, here's twenty dollars. Go up to the drugstore and buy ten combs, ten pair of scissors, and ten tweezers. If they cost too much, buy as much as you can." Dad glanced over at Sheila and Joan who were at the kitchen table finishing their French toast breakfast and said, "And take your sisters with you." The twenty-minute walk to the drugstore felt like an eternity. We didn't giggle and skip like we sometimes did. Silent, each of us were alone in our own thoughts. It was clear that something was wrong with Dad, and I felt sure I was to blame, which he seemed to validate by giving me the twenty dollars to and ordering me to go to the drugstore.

Sheila, Joan, and I made the trip together. With our heads hung low, we walked to the intersection where the drug store was located.

It had no crossing signal, and we waited until both sides of the street were clear of cars. With lightning speed and hands clasped, we made a mad dash to the other side.

We snuck in the back door of the drugstore and tiptoed through the aisles, whispering so nobody would hear us. I didn't want any questions about what we were looking for. Feeling self-conscious, I sensed heat spread to my face. Joan and I pretended we were looking at the pearl earrings on the counter when a salesperson strolled by. I searched through the comb aisle and found the ones Dad liked. It had to be a specific black comb, a row of small teeth on one end and larger teeth at the other end. They had only five of this type of comb, so I grabbed all five. I had no idea whether this would be enough to make him happy, but I desperately hoped so. We'd watched him go crazy the night before, and I worried he'd do it again if we didn't get it right. Next, I found five pair of tweezers. I calculated the cost of everything and decided we had enough money to buy all five pairs of scissors with plenty leftover. We cleaned the store out of these items.

At the register, my internal shame made me feel like I was going to explode. My face had to be a wild strawberry color. I was hot and sweating and avoided making eye contact with the cashier. There was a small food area off to the side of the store and a counter where people stood eating and drinking. A couple sat there, casually eating French fries and sipping milkshakes. "Why can't we do that?" I said to my sister.

"Because Dad would kill us if we'd used the money for that!" she said. *Someday when I get older*, I thought, *I am going to sit at the counter like a normal person. I will order a chocolate milkshake and dream of what my life will be.*

I understand now that this was the first time outside our home that I'd felt shame and embarrassment over my father's behavior. It would not be the last. My internalized shame became the lens through which all my future experiences would be perceived. I became withdrawn and self-conscious. I blushed easily and acquired the label of "shy."

By the time I was fourteen, I started acting out. I developed an "I don't care about anything" attitude. Although I was crumbling inside, my exterior was tough. I made friends that had the same "I don't give a shit" attitude, and I started smoking cigarettes and tried smoking pot for the first time. I became a headstrong teenager who ignored all school policies and skipped an entire week of school at the beginning of my freshman year which led to a three-day suspension.

Mom explained away Dad's behavior. Each time our drunken father would traumatize his children, our mother would tell us that he was sorry and wouldn't do it again. She was lying.

Because I asked questions, I was labeled the "overly sensitive" one. And because Dad "didn't mean it," I wasn't supposed to get upset. But I wondered why I was the only one who seemed worried. What if there was something terribly wrong with Dad? He'd never acted like this before. I just wanted to talk about my feelings and what was going on, but no one in my family wanted to listen.

"Susan, why are you so sensitive?" Mom would ask whenever I brought up something that was weighing on my mind. My sisters eventually started calling me sensitive, too, and then teased me about it. "Oh, Susan, why do you have to be so—so sensitive?"

Eventually I stopped asking questions.

Those middle-of-the night interruptions didn't stop, and we were dispatched to the drugstore a few more times after Mom promised it wouldn't happen again. Before long, my mother said, "Next time your dad wakes you up, try to ignore his yelling." I learned that when I did indeed ignore him, he'd eventually stop yelling, and sooner or later he'd pass out.

~∞~

DAD WAS VERY different on Cape Cod. Every July our family made the four-hour trip from our home in Springfield, Massachusetts, to spend one glorious week in Wellfleet, Massachusetts, located at the eastern tip of the state on the Atlantic Ocean. Each year, at least a week before the trip, the beige, round suitcase my grandmother had given me sat in my bedroom packed and ready to go. Dad would wake us at the crack of dawn with, "Rise and shine, kids, we're going to the Cape!" Just like on Christmas morning, the excitement masked our weariness at the early hour.

To avoid any arguments, my mom told each of us where we'd be sitting in the car. Mom and Dad sat up front, Dad driving. The youngest ones—Charles, Mary, and Margaret—usually sat in the middle seat wearing lap belts. Sheila and I sat in the third row, which we called the "way back" and which had no seat belts. We'd put the entire seat down, spread out a couple of blankets, and add our pillows. We'd lie on our stomachs facing the back window and wave at passersby, then giggle with delight whenever one waved back.

Because there was no more room in the station wagon, two kids had to travel with my grandmother in her car. She was always included in our week-long vacation, and everyone wanted to ride with her. We all thought her car was the coolest, a 1962 white Chevy Impala convertible with red leather seats. Marie always got to sit in the front seat because she was the oldest. Every year, either Sheila, Joan, or I would be allowed to sit in the back seat. This year it was Joan's turn. The first stop was always the gas station, then the local drugstore where we'd stock up on a week's worth of comic books and an extra deck of playing cards.

At the first sighting of the Sagamore Bridge, which crossed over the Cape Cod canal, the Archie, Betty & Veronica, and Richie Rich comic books were tossed on the floor of the station wagon. "Look, there's the bridge!" Dad always said. Crossing the bridge that connected Cape Cod with the rest of Massachusetts meant that we were officially on "the Cape," as the locals called it. My sisters and brother and I would strain our necks to get a peek of the water from the car window as we drove over it. There were a lot of *oohs* and *aahs*, and the car was abuzz with the same kind of excitement we felt when Jim, the ice cream truck driver, pulled up in front of our house. We were a lively bunch in the back seats of the Chevy station wagon, happily anticipating what the week might bring.

Wellfleet's cool summer morning air was typically filled with light mists redolent of salt. The sun frequently made its presence known by lunchtime after the fog had burned off, and this always meant warm beach days for us followed by summer nights cool enough that we needed sweatshirts. At home summer nights were muggy, and even with the windows open it was hot. But I always slept well on Cape Cod, even on my little cot. There were no night-mares and no middle-of-the-night tirades from my dad. Cape Cod seemed sacred, and even today, it remains a peaceful haven for me. I thank my mother's mother for that. Perhaps it was her being with us for the week that made my dad behave so differently. Maybe he re-spected her. Maybe he even hoped that Cape Cod would help him find a way to stop drinking. Whatever it was, I enjoyed that disparity and wished we could stay there forever.

My favorite thing to do on the Cape was go to the beach and search for seashells and tiny white rocks along the water's edge as I dug my feet in the sand. And I loved to eat the fish and chips and homemade ice cream that seemed like the area's native cuisine. The sandy dunes that lined the edges of the beach were our playground, and my siblings and I ran freely, playing tag and tumbling around on the soft sand. We saw lighthouses, sailboats, lobsters, and real fisher-men. Natural and man-made beauty was everywhere.

Our cottage was located on a dead-end street that curved around and ended at a large salt marsh where my dad took us to dig for clams. One of my most vivid memories of that street is of the trees. I loved the fifty-foot pitch pine trees with their twisted drooping branches and thick, dark-grey bark, the even taller white pines with abundant bluish-green needles, and my favorite, the short, stocky trunks and widespread branches of the white oaks that lined the sides of the sandy dirt road. The smell of pine needles and salt permeated the air. Similar cottages were scattered along the road, peeking through the woods. Station wagons with open trunks sat idling on broken seashell driveways, unloading for the week. And every year, family photos were snapped under the pine trees in front of the cottages.

Dad was happy here. In the early days, he was never drunk on vacation. He wore his favorite madras or seersucker shorts and colorful Oxford shirts. No folded-with-medium-starch laundered dress shirts or wingtips here. Always comfortable shirts and loafers or boat shoes. He spent his time on a beach chair under a beach umbrella, reading magazines, books, and the daily newspaper. He would drink a beer or two and swim with us. Some years he drank only root beer. I didn't understand then what "on the wagon" meant, but what I did know was that it represented carefree summers for me. No worrying, no unpredictability, no parents arguing, and normal bedtime routines.

Dad was more generous on Cape Cod, too. One year when we pulled up to the Wellfleet General Store, down the street from our cottage, I had my eye on a red-and-blue water raft that hung on a steel clothesline outside the store. It was the perfect size to ride waves. "Dad, can we buy one of those? Please, pretty please?" I begged. After my siblings and I agreed to take turns sharing, he bought two of them.

There were two beaches we went to on a regular basis. We called them "the one with the big waves"—on the ocean side—and "the one with the little waves"—on the bay side. The bay side was not my favorite, but I had to put up with going there for the sake of the little ones. The oyster shells that lined the bay's floor made it hard to maneuver in and out of the water without cutting our feet on sharp oyster-shell edges. My favorite beach was called Lecount Hollow. Although the water was always colder on the Atlantic Ocean side, I loved the softness of the sandy ocean floor, and I'd happily ride the rolling waves on my raft. We were like yo-yos, springing back and forth from the beach blanket to the water all day long. We'd call out, "Mom, Dad, watch this!" And my heart warmed my chilly body whenever my parents sat together near the water in their beach chairs and watched us ride the waves.

Every time our Cape week ended, I dreaded going home. I wanted to stay on Cape Cod forever. I felt carefree there. Our family was happy there. Our dad was kind there, and we were allowed to let go and actually have fun with him. On vacation, he was both laid-back and upbeat. My parents were cheerful together on Cape Cod, and I wanted them to be like that always. The Cape was our dream place where everything was perfect, and the glow from a week in Wellfleet even extended for a while after we returned to Springfield.

Then, the year I turned fifteen, even the Cape experience went sour. During the drive home that year, my mom told my dad to pull over. "You're drunk," she commanded. "Stop this car. I'm driving."

CHAPTER 3

JUNE 2007

$\mathcal{F}$our days after my mammogram and three days after the ultrasound that all but confirmed my cancer diagnosis, I traveled to St. Louis with my sister Mary to close on my new house. Bruce stayed home because it was the last week of his fellowship, and he wasn't able to get time off. That he was able to stay home and do some fun weekend things with Samantha soothed my anxious heart. Mary and I were thrilled to be spending time together. Although recent events had left me melancholy, being with my sister always felt like a gift. We lived three hours apart, and other than the occasional Thanksgiving or Easter dinner, we weren't able to see each other as much as we wanted. Over the past twenty years, parenting had been all-consuming for both of us, and one-on-one sister time was rare.

It was a beautiful peacock-blue-sky day, the kind of day when I didn't mind flying. I'd always get a window seat and gaze at the beauty below. There was something magical about looking out at the vastness, the open blue sky, the white puffy clouds, and the cars below that looked like fast-moving ants. I saw a housing development with spacious, beautiful homes and focused on one house with a large built-in pool whose blue water sparkled in the brightness of the sun. Two cars in the driveway. I wondered if a woman lived there. Perhaps she also had breast cancer. At this point the cancer was only a "maybe," but I could already see how it had changed me. Looking down from that plane, I told myself that I'd never judge anyone again because I have no idea what others are going through. All those people below, all the houses, the buildings, and the bustling traffic. The problems that I realized must exist in those lives made my own malignant growth seem small.

Mary and I had never flown together before, and on takeoff we gripped hands, squeezed tight for a second, and smiled at each other. During the flight we caught up on each other's lives. We were so absorbed in our conversation that the other two hundred or so people aboard the plane seemed nonexistent, and before we knew it, we were landing.

Once in St. Louis, we went straight to our hotel. It was a hot June day, already muggy and in the high eighties. The pool was inviting with its aquamarine-meets-sea-green color, and we decided to make lounging by it our first order of business.

We grabbed two white towels from the bin located next to the entry gate and set up camp on a pair of woven chaise lounges. Then we sat at the edge of the pool with our legs dangling in the perfectly cool water. I let out a relaxed sigh. It had been over a year since my last break from my job at Yale New Haven Hospital. I was relaxed until the water in the pool started creating small waves around us, stirred up by our legs swinging back and forth in water up to our knees. A scene that had been serene turned suddenly ominous, reminding me of the cancerous monster wave that was building up momentum and getting ready to crash on my shore.

Panic rose in my throat. My biggest fear was likely coming true. I just knew I had breast cancer! I decided I had to tell Mary something I'd never shared with anyone. I'd been afraid of getting breast cancer since I was about ten years old—when I'd first found out about my grandmother's breast cancer. And, now that fear was most likely going to become my own reality.

∽✺∾

MY GRANDMOTHER, WHOM I called "Grammie Golden," was diagnosed with breast cancer in 1944 at age thirty-seven. Chemotherapy wasn't even an option then. She endured a radical double mastectomy along with radiation, which left her both flat-chested and with deep depressions in her chest, especially on the right side, where they removed all her lymph nodes and surrounding tissue. She wasn't ashamed of this disfigurement, though, and she'd show me her scars whenever I'd asked her to.

She wore a normal bra stuffed full of Kleenex and with a Catholic prayer medal pinned to it. Now I wondered if she'd ever felt a weird tingling like I had. Growing up, I used to wonder, *why her?* and now I couldn't help but wonder, *why me?*

MY SISTER MARIE was twelve years old when she started developing what my mother called "breast buds." When my mom took Marie shopping for her first bra, Sheila and I stuffed our shirts with tissues and strutted around the house, pretending we were already developed. I already knew by age ten that my breasts would get bigger— and I wanted "boobies!" But because of Grammie Golden, I was also aware that boobies could be cut off, and that possibility terrified me. That night, I added an additional prayer to my nighttime routine: "Please God, don't let me get my boobies cut off like Grammie's."

The image of my grandmother's scarred chest where her breasts had been haunted me. And I believe it made an impact on my decision-making, possibly even unconsciously as I grew into young adulthood. I tried to incorporate into my life things that I'd heard would lower my cancer risk: I had my first two kids at twenty-three and twenty-five, breastfed all my children, quit smoking at age twenty-two, and started regularly exercising at age twenty-five. My personal risk was actually no higher than normal because it was my grandmother and not a first degree relative like my mother who'd had the disease. But I didn't know that at the time. I lived in the shadow of that fear.

After I finished sharing my fear of getting breast cancer, Mary turned to me and said,

"Well, maybe it will turn out to be nothing." Mary told me about a friend of hers who'd recently had a breast biopsy and was convinced that she had breast cancer. "But it was negative," she said. "That could happen to you, too. It might turn out that you're worrying about nothing. Let's just try not to think about it, okay?"

I told her about the mammogram, ultrasound, and my appointment with the oncologist, and how it sure didn't seem like it was going to turn out to be nothing. How I'd looked into their eyes for a flicker of reassurance to keep my hope alive but had come away empty-handed. And my intuition was nagging me. I told her about the biopsy that was scheduled for the upcoming week. She said she'd always viewed me as the strong one, ever since we were little. "No matter what happens," she said, "I know you'll be able to handle it. I'll come to St. Louis to help you. If you have to have chemo, I'll come with you." It was a relief to talk to my sister about all that was happening and to feel I was not alone. My shoulders relaxed. Slightly.

I had a meeting later that afternoon with my attorney and the realtor. I signed all the necessary paperwork and acquired the deed that would make Bruce and me homeowners in St. Louis.

When I had the keys in hand, Mary and I got into our red Chevy Cruz rental car, plugged my new address into the GPS, and drove to my new home.

The entrance to Woodcliff Heights was located at the end of a curvy road, similar to the rolling country roads of Farmington. Plum-colored redbud trees flanked the sizeable, stone-encased subdivision sign. Eight white dogwood trees in full bloom lined each side of the ascending hill. The brick-front, traditional Tudor-style home that sat second house on the right was all mine.

We pulled the rental car into the concrete driveway and parked in front of the three-car garage. Out front a sign that read SOLD in big white letters stood at attention on the lawn. Mary and I walked along the curved concrete sidewalk that led to the front door. Standing at the arched front entrance, looking up at a black glass lantern that hung above the embossed glass front door, I thought about Bruce. I missed him and wished he were here. I imagined him lifting me over the threshold like a newlywed, and the thought of it brought a smile to my face. He'd done this with every new home we'd moved into, and I loved the tradition. We'd been married sixteen years, but sometimes it felt as if we were newlyweds.

Mary and I walked through the expansive two-story house, stopping at times to pose for photos. I entered the master suite and stopped to admire the coffered ceiling as thoughts of breast cancer and surgeries and procedures interrupted my homeowner fantasies. I thought about the treatments I'd likely have to endure for breast cancer if the biopsy came back positive. They could be brutal, I'd heard. Most likely, I'd be staring at the ceiling a lot. I made a note to buy some lavender candles for the bedroom. The scent of lavender always soothed my soul.

We canvassed the neighborhood by car and then stopped for lunch at an outdoor stone patio bar that the realtor had noted was one of the nicest restaurants in the area. Closing my eyes, enjoying the strong Midwestern sun, I thought about how keyed-up I'd been about this new chapter of my life with Bruce, and now it was being interrupted by something potentially enormous and menacing. Cancer hunched over my mind like the beast it is.

Ever since I'd had the mammogram, my life had been moving too fast, and I felt as if I couldn't catch my breath. I was moving 1,500 miles away from my family, children, and my friends just when I needed them most, and I felt emotionally vulnerable.

I had to believe that no matter how difficult things became, I had been placed on this path for a reason. I thought about God and my Catholic upbringing. I'd grown up with a punitive God. There were no rewards, only sins. As a child, I had prayed nightly and attended church and CCD classes every Sunday. That stopped when I was sixteen. The God I'd been praying to wasn't helping me. If God was supposed to help people, why hadn't he listened to me and answered my prayers about my dad? Where was he when I'd needed him?

After two relatively relaxing days in St. Louis, I was back home in Connecticut and psychologically preparing myself for the biopsy. I was feeling pretty melancholy at this point but eager to know the details of the procedure. I logged onto my computer and started an internet search. I'd always believed that knowledge is power, but this time knowledge turned out to be perplexity. After more than three hours online, I had learned everything imaginable about breast biopsies, but instead of feeling better, I came away stumped because I didn't have any of the precursors for cancer. And I really wanted to find a cause. I became fixated on figuring out the "Why Me?"

Bruce and Sam's laughing snapped me out of my trance. Bruce called out, "Come on down, Sue, you have to watch this movie with us—it is sooo funny." It was *Anchorman*, and Bruce knew that I loved Will Ferrell. I needed a laugh right about then, so I saved my results and logged off my computer with every intention of getting back on to do more searching in the morning.

Monday morning arrived—biopsy day. Unable to sleep, I pulled back my white down comforter at five in the morning and sat at the edge of my bed. Feeling the heavy load of the day, I cradled my forehead in both hands.

I put on my light-blue Natori bathrobe and a pair of clean white cotton socks and proceeded downstairs to the kitchen. The biopsy was scheduled for ten o'clock, and as the coffee brewed, I looked out the kitchen window into the blackness of the backyard. Pitch-darkness always conjured scary images in my mind. It reminded me of my childhood, a place without light where danger always lurked.

Bruce and Sam were still sound asleep. With coffee in hand, I climbed up the stairs quietly to the second floor. Before I sat at my oak wraparound desk, I peeked in Sam's room. She was sleeping like a baby lamb, all covered up in her purple-and-pink flowered comforter. Just the sight of her made me smile. I enjoyed the quiet of the morning, even with Bruce's light snoring coming from the adjacent room.

After taking a deep inhale of my hazelnut coffee, I logged on to the internet and typed into the search bar, "What are the risk factors of getting breast cancer?" A tidy, vertical list appeared near the top of my screen:

Being overweight

Lack of exercise

Smoking cigarettes

Eating unhealthy foods

Having a first child after age thirty

Breast-feeding may lower your risk, especially if you breast feed longer than one year.

I didn't have any of those risk factors. I wasn't overweight, and I'd just taken up yoga. I'd had my first child at age twenty-three and breast-fed all three of my kids, two of them for over a year. I had even started eating organic fruits and vegetables.

I scrolled down to another statistic: Eighty percent of breast cancers are caused by environmental factors. My curious nature took over and kept digging.

I felt as if I were back in nursing school as I researched medical journals in psychology, psychiatry, family medicine, and women's health. I landed on links, including,

"Childhood Family Violence History and Women's Risk for Intimate Partner Violence and Poor Health."

"Adverse Childhood Experiences and the Presence of Cancer Risk Factors in Adulthood."

"Health Related Outcomes of Adverse Childhood Experiences."

"Correlates of Adverse Childhood Experiences Among Adults with Severe Mood Disorder."

Bleary-eyed after two hours of searching, I'd read enough articles on stress and cancer to have convinced myself that this was the cause I'd been looking for. I'd read about the difference between acute and chronic stress and how prolonged stresses can negatively affect one's physical and mental being. I hadn't heard the term "Adverse Childhood Experiences" before. Was this what I'd lived through as a child —adverse experiences?

I knew that stress was generally bad news and could even make people sick, but I never knew it could cause a major illness. My job was stressful, but that was acute stress. The chronic stress I'd suffered as a child was likely a much larger factor. That morning I learned that traumas become internalized and remain forever painful and present. The body does indeed remember, as I'd come to learn many years later by reading Bessel van der Kolk's book *The Body Keeps the Score*, and Donna Jackson Nakazawa's book *Childhood Disrupted*. Both books would become like bibles for me—for living life after trauma.

As it turns out, the culprit is cortisol, the "stress hormone," which is produced by the adrenal glands through signals from the pituitary and the hypothalamus. When someone is in "fight or flight" mode, as when the body deems it is in danger, cortisol levels elevate. Cortisol has positive functions, too, but the negative impacts of being flooded with the hormone over time are very real. Holy shit! This was my smoking gun! A cortisol war.

I logged off the computer when Bruce and Samantha woke up around eight. We hadn't told Sam what was happening, and at thirteen years old, I didn't think she should have to worry about me. I put on a smile and sat with her while she ate breakfast. "Have a great day," I said as I kissed her and gave her a good-bye hug. Bruce drove her to the school bus stop.

I was convinced that my childhood was to blame for my anxiety and depression. Now I suspected that my parents' stormy marriage, my father's alcoholic behavior, and the chronic stress in my childhood contributed to my cancer diagnosis.

Two hours later, Dr. Zimmerman performed the biopsy. In a supine position, my legs quivering, I stared at the same spot on the ceiling that I'd watched when I'd had the ultrasound. There was some pulling, some pinching and then, with the sound of a click, a piece of my breast tissue was removed. Off to the lab it went.

The following weekend, less than a week after my biopsy, I boarded a three-hour flight to Orlando to attend a nursing conference. The Association of Women's Health, Obstetric and Neonatal Nurses (AWHONN) conference happened once a year in my nursing specialty, and I'd been planning to go with my friend Ellen from work. I didn't want a possible diagnosis to stand in my way, so I kept my plan. Following my sister Mary's lead, I kept repeating to myself, "It just might be nothing." Ellen and I had planned to meet in the hotel lobby. We'd both been looking forward to getting away from the craziness at work and spending some time together. Little did she know how much I needed the distraction.

I arrived in Orlando, home to Mickey Mouse and Gatorworld, on a blindingly bright 82-degree June day. Back home, I knew Bruce was concerned about me, so I decided to call him to let him know I'd arrived safely. But my cell phone was nowhere to be found. Sitting on my bed in the hotel room, I reached over, picked up the hotel phone, and dialed home. Bruce answered and, before I even asked, said, "You forgot your phone. It's sitting on the kitchen counter."

I knew I'd been distracted, but this pointed to just how much this biopsy was weighing on me. I never went anywhere without my phone, and especially not to another state.

"I'm going to mail it to you," Bruce said. We both knew I'd need it when my doctor called with the biopsy results. Bruce told me he'd drop it off at FedEx and I'd have it the next morning. I didn't know whether to be gloomy or grateful.

Ellen and I met up in the lobby near a sign for the hotel's spa, and I scheduled an Ayurvedic facial for the following morning. Then she and I headed to the bar for a few drinks.

The following morning's facial was everything I needed, and I emerged relaxed. As I walked to the conference center to pick up my phone, I enjoyed the beautiful red hibiscus flowers that lined the path. My hands were shaking as I opened the FedEx package. My phone beeped to indicate that a voicemail was waiting.

My stomach did flip flops. It was a Connecticut number, one I didn't recognize. Like a bull, my thoughts ran wild. I listened to the message from my oncologist, Dr. Ayer, once, then twice, then three times and still had no sense of reassurance. Her voice was flat, and the message said simply that she had the results of my breast biopsy and that I needed to call her back. After that Bruce called. He said, "Call her right now, and then call me back."

I found a quiet area and dialed the return number with trembling fingers. Dr. Ayer answered on the second ring. "Susan, I am sorry to say that your biopsy results came back positive for carcinoma."

Unconsciously, my body reacted by rocking back and forth. It was a movement I'd repeated many times when comforting my babies. My mouth went dry, and bile seemed to snake its way up my throat.

My greatest fear had just been realized. I'd kept my secret so buried that I hadn't even believed it until I'd spoken of it out loud to my sister. I had fucking breast cancer. Trembling from head to toe, I asked her what I should do now; she told me to get myself home, to call her office in the morning, and that we'd set up an appointment to discuss the biopsy results. I then ended the phone call and started searching for somewhere to sit. I wished Bruce were here to catch me. The fight-or-flight response took over my body. I was on the verge of hyperventilating, and I felt lightheaded. "Oh my God," I said aloud. Afraid I was going to pass out, I tried to ground myself and stop my racing thoughts. *What the fuck am I supposed to do now? What does one do when she is told she has cancer?* I wanted to go home.

Trying to conceal my panic and tears, I made my way back to my hotel room. Sobbing uncontrollably, I threw myself face first onto the bed. Once the initial terror subsided and my crying slowed, I called Ellen. She knew I'd been waiting for some news from my doctor, and she dropped everything and came to my room. She helped me check out of the hotel and change my flight. I remember nothing of the trip to the airport or the flight home. All I know is that Bruce was there to pick me up when I landed.

CHAPTER 4

1972

A distinct smell of smoke woke me up in the middle of the night. I thought I'd been dreaming when my eyes popped open and I gasped for air. I bolted up in bed as my eyes skimmed the darkened room. I was fifteen, and my twin sister was sound asleep in the bed next to mine. An eerie feeling rushed over me. I wasn't dreaming. Something was definitely burning.

Because we didn't have a fireplace, I was immediately alert. The smell had to be coming from downstairs. Wary, I left the comfort of my bed and walked barefoot along the green shag carpeting to the stairs. I lingered at the top step, breathing in and trying to figure out what the smell was. What the heck was going on downstairs? I was afraid to find out.

I'd gone down those stairs many times in the middle of the night, always at my father's drunken insistence. "Get up!" he'd bark, and my sisters and I would startle awake and march down the stairs together, filled with dread. There were times when I brought along my doll for safety. But this night was different—no one was yelling. The entire house was quiet. Even my parents were still asleep in their first-floor bedroom. I checked the clock at the top of the stairs: two in the morning.

The smell bombarded my nostrils as I made my way down the stairs, which eventually landed me in the living room. There in the middle of the room, sitting cross-legged, yoga-style on the floor, was my seventeen-year-old sister Marie. I gasped, "What the hell?" A grapefruit-sized spot of the shaggy green carpet was on fire, short little flames shooting upward about six inches.

Marie, with her long, tangled brown hair covering her face, sat in front of her miniature bonfire, perfectly calm, just holding a lighter. Then she flicked the lighter to life, pressing the little flame to the carpet fibers. The fire in the reflection of her eyes made her look possessed. Despite my growing agitation, she didn't seem aware that I was standing there.

IT WAS ON a night in Cape Cod two months earlier that I first noticed something weird was happening to Marie. It was a typically cool Cape Cod summer evening as I walked out of the cottage and into the pitch black to empty the trash. My eyes took several seconds to adjust to the blackness, and then I saw Marie sitting on the grass smoking a cigarette her back propped against a large tree trunk. The dark wool blanket we used for the beach was wrapped around her head and shoulders, and she hugged her knees into her chest. The sky was ablaze with white stars, and the sounds of crickets echoed in the distant field. As I walked closer to my sister, I could see that she was shaking her head from side to side; it was as if she were trying to shake away whatever was going on inside her head. She was shivering even though she was wrapped in that big blanket. She puffed intently on her cigarette leaving the ash hanging low. The closer I got, the creepier she looked.

"Marie what are you doing there? You scared me."

"I'm having a flashback."

I thought flashbacks happened only to people returning from the Vietnam War. "What do you mean by 'a flashback'?" I asked.

"I took some LSD last week, and now I keep having these weird flashbacks."

She then told me she'd gone to a party a few days earlier, and her friend had put acid in her lemonade drink without her knowing.

"What is a flashback like?"

"It's really scary—don't ever do acid, Susan. I see scary things in my mind."

"Like what, for example?"

"It's like having a nightmare—but you're awake."

"What do you want me to do? Do you want me to get Mom?" I asked.

"No, I'll be okay. I just have to wait until it passes."

I didn't care what Marie said. I went back into the cottage and found my mother in the kitchen boiling lobster for my dad.

"Mom, Marie is sitting outside all alone in the dark, and she seems scared. She said she's is having a flashback"

"Did she use that word? Flashback?" my mother asked.

"Yes—that's what she called it."

My mom's eyes widened, and in a higher pitch than usual she said, "Oh my God, did she do drugs? You only get flashbacks when you do drugs."

"I don't know, Mom, but she seems really scared."

As I watched over the boiling lobster, my mother went outside to talk to Marie. She returned a very short time later.

"Is she going to be okay?" I asked.

"I hope so." My mom said. "This happened once before. It passed. Marie just wants to be alone right now."

I stared at my mother, expecting her to have more to say about this disturbing episode with her daughter. But she seemed unmoved. "It's a good thing that we're going home tomorrow," she said.

After we returned from Cape Cod, Marie's behavior got progressively worse. She began sleeping in more and more and started missing days of school. I was surprised because this was her senior year. I thought she'd be excited. Eventually she stopped going altogether.

Marie used to care about what she looked like, but by this point she wasn't showering or changing her clothes. Her once-beautiful hair was disheveled and clumped into a knot at the back of her head. Days and weeks went by. She spent her days sitting crossed leg style on the living room floor or sofa for hours at a time mumbling to herself. When she did speak, her sentences were baffling.

By Halloween, Marie receded further into herself, sequestered in her room for days. Her acoustic guitar sat alone in the corner of her room. Withdrawn and paranoid, she started having hallucinations. The paranoia made her think she was being followed by the FBI and that people were stealing from her. She started picking fights with all of us, started sleeping less and less, and then she stopped communicating completely.

BACK IN THE living room, Marie's eyes had the same kind of lifeless look I'd seen that night on Cape Cod. This night was different, though. She didn't speak a word. Instinctively, I rushed toward her, grabbed the lighter and cigarettes out her hands, and shoved her away from the fire with all my might. "Marie, what the hell are you doing?" I cried out, as if suddenly coming to my senses. "Are you freaking nuts?" I was terrified to feel that her body was stiff as a corpse, but I grabbed a pillow from the nearby sofa and pounded the flames. Leaving the pillow to cover the smoldering fire, I ran into the kitchen and returned with a large glass of water. I lifted the pillow and heaved the water onto the scorched spot, which was now the size of a watermelon. After repeating this one more time, I opened the small window in the living room. When the cold air blew in, Marie didn't flinch, blink, or even move a muscle. She was still lying in the position I'd pushed her into, staring into space, staring at nothing, motionless and rigid. Sweat pooled between my breasts, bile lurked in my throat, and I felt like vomiting. I pushed Marie back into a seated position. Like a statue, she stayed right where I positioned her. I didn't yet know the meaning of the word "catatonic," but I knew something was very seriously wrong with her. She was like a zombie, and I was petrified.

Alone and confused, I walked into the kitchen and sat down at the table. I thought of waking up my mom to tell her what just happened, but my gut told me that she wouldn't do anything to help.

Since returning from our vacation on Cape Cod, I'd been complaining about Marie and her odd behavior, but each time my mother's response was the same: "I know, Susan, I just don't know what to do about it right now." She'd even shared with me that my dad was fighting her about getting Marie help. I didn't know anything about mental illness, but I did know that Marie wasn't getting better and I suspected that might mean that she needed to be hospitalized. It was silent throughout the house, so I decided to go back to bed and tell my mother in the morning.

I'd just put out a fire that could have destroyed our entire home and killed us all. The reality of this tried to work its way into my young brain as I climbed the stairs to my bedroom, holding onto the railing to steady myself. It was, after all, a school night, and I had to wake up early. I climbed back into bed and covered my legs with my blanket. I glanced over at Sheila's bed, which was right next to mine. Only a small brown desk separated my bed from Sheila's, and I could see that she was beginning to stir. She opened her eyes, and I blurted, "Marie just started a freaking fire in the living room."

"She what?"

"I woke up to the smell of smoke, so I went downstairs and found Marie sitting in the middle of the living room burning the freaking rug with a cigarette!"

"Oh, my God, you're kidding me. Did you put it out?" she asked.

"Yes."

"Are you sure?"

"Yeah, I poured water on it to make sure it was out."

"You have to tell Mom," Sheila said. "Marie's freaking nuts."

"Yeah, I guess, maybe in the morning."

"What's Marie doing now?" Sheila asked.

"I have no idea. She's probably still sitting there where I left her. Something is seriously wrong with her." Hearing these words come out of my mouth confirmed what I knew to be true, that I believed my sister Marie was going crazy. I was baffled but knew that her behavior wasn't just about a flashback. What had made her stiff as an ironing board and immobile? Although I was scared, I was also sad. This, whatever it was, was happening to my big sister, and my heart was breaking for her. I desperately wanted her to get help.

As a family, we were stuck, and I questioned why my parents weren't doing anything to help Marie. We were all witnessing Marie's descent into hell and were afraid of what would happen next. I'd stopped praying for the last few weeks because the prayers weren't helping and seemed futile. Nothing had changed. My dad's drinking was escalating at an alarming rate, and I was still afraid every day. Where was God in all this? Nobody else would listen to me, so in my desperation, I prayed anyway. Lying in bed, curled up in a fetal position, I prayed to God, the angels, and anyone else out there that could help my family. My mom used to use the phrase, "Jesus, Mary, and Joseph," whenever she was upset. I tried them too, and all the other holy saints I'd learned about in all those years of catechism. *Please, someone, anyone, help me and my family. We're coming apart at the seams. I'm afraid that something really bad is going to happen. I'm afraid that Marie is going to kill us all while we sleep. Please, God, let us all not die tonight.* When I ran out of prayers, I fell back to sleep.

The next morning, before I left to catch the school bus, I told my mother what had happened during the night. I brought her into the living room and showed her the giant burn mark in the center of the room. In unison, her mouth and eyes opened wide. When she asked me why I hadn't woken her up, I hesitated but then confessed, "I figured you wouldn't do anything about it. You're just letting Marie rot."

My mother said, "That's not true, Susan. Something will be done, whether your father likes it or not."

But I wasn't buying any of it. Somewhere deep in my gut, my soul, my unconscious—somewhere—I knew that this was the beginning of the end of my family as I knew it.

I couldn't have known at the time the emotional and psychological impact this fire incident would have on me. There I was, a girl at fifteen, and already I'd become like a tortoise with a hard outer shell that shielded me from feeling emotion. Nobody understood. Nobody helped. And subsequently, I lost the ability to feel anything, including happiness or pleasure, until well into my thirties. I'd come to learn that unexpressed emotions never die; they are buried alive and will emerge later in uglier ways.

The next day, my mother took my sister to a local hospital, and she was admitted into the mental health care unit.

*A*s I faced the diagnosis of breast cancer, the same massive dark cloud that had settled itself over my home as a teenager hovered like a funnel cloud above me.

Something was triggered in me the night before my appointment with Dr. Ayer, and I started rocking myself to sleep. I began to feel the kind of terror I'd felt during the fire with Marie and during my father's drunken rages. The nightmares, the fear, the angst, the pain, the sadness, the grief, and the loss of dreams—all of it was back. The past was showing up in my present, fast and furious. I had no idea what to expect from this cancer.

Back in Dr. Ayer's office, we discussed the results of the biopsy. Infiltrating ductal carcinoma of the breast was what they called it. The tumor was 1.6 centimeters and in Stage 1. She said it was mitotically active (high-grade cancer), which meant it was growing at a fast rate and had a high recurrence rate. It was estrogen positive which meant the tumor's food was estrogen. Dr. Ayer told me that usually anything under two centimeters didn't require chemotherapy, but mine was so aggressive that she was recommending it. All estrogen would be removed from my body, automatically sending my body into early menopause.

My mind shuddered when I heard the word menopause. I imagined hot flashes and other physical changes I associated with being an old lady: would I also become thick around the middle? Would my skin begin to sag? Would every part of me begin to dry? Those were the garden-variety thoughts that plagued me. And then, there were the medical words that now invaded my life: mitotically active, high grade, Estrogen receptor-positive (ER+) and Progesterone receptor-positive (PR+), Oncotype testing, chemotherapy, steroid drugs, Taxotere, Cytoxan, aromatase inhibitors, anti-estrogen therapy, genetic testing, Nottingham score, metaplasia, port-a-cath. But mostly I was terrified of chemotherapy. I'd tried to imagine what was in store for me: vomiting, losing my hair, looking like I was at death's door. I wondered what I'd look like bald. I felt like a passenger in a car being driven by cancer. I wasn't in control, and that bugged the shit out of me. I never liked unpredictability.

A plan was devised, and all I had to do was sign on. It was clear-cut and involved sentinel node biopsy; surgery, either a mastectomy or lumpectomy (my choice); four rounds of chemotherapy; thirty-three days of radiation; and five years of the anti-estrogen drug tamoxifen. The only hitch was that the surgery would happen in Connecticut, and due to our impending move, the rest of my treatment, which included chemotherapy and radiation, would continue in St. Louis.

I liked how Dr. Ayer took her time explaining things to Bruce and me. She drew pictures that illustrated what was going on inside my breast. Being a visual person, that helped me understand it all. She had a patient and friendly manner that kept me feeling calm. I really trusted her. After discussing surgical options with her, I flashed back to the image of my grandmother's breasts after her mastectomy and began to panic again. I wanted my breast preserved as much as possible. Dr. Ayer proposed a lumpectomy, explaining that in my situation, there was no long-term benefit to having a mastectomy. I felt a moment of relief.

To minimize the risk of recurrence, I still needed the chemotherapy and radiation after the surgery. But first up was the surgery, which needed to happen right away. I'd have to find an oncologist in

St. Louis, but that seemed like a world away. And whoever it was would hopefully agree with the proposed plan. Knowing little about cancer, I had to trust my current team led by Dr. Ayer. The hospital in Connecticut was a teaching hospital, and I knew that teaching hospitals tend to be on top of their game. They have all the recent data, studies, and new advances at the tips of their fingers. It occurred to me that I probably should get a second opinion, but there wasn't time for one. And though I trusted Dr. Ayer, I couldn't stop the silent question that kept popping up in my brain: What if I was making the wrong decision?

Trusting had been difficult for me in the past, but at this point of my cancer journey, I needed to take a risk and trust in the unknown. My life depended on it.

The week my doctor wanted to schedule the surgery was the same week we'd planned to take our yearly vacation to Martha's Vineyard. The choices presented to me were to postpone the surgery a week and keep my vacation or to schedule the surgery during that week and cancel the trip that we'd planned over six months ago. I didn't think a week would make a difference in the long run. I chose the vacation, and I felt my entire body sigh with relief as the car boarded the ferry to the island. Bruce, Sam, and I drove together in our car. My daughter Sarah, now a schoolteacher in her late twenties and her wonderful husband, John, would join us there in a few days. A year and a half earlier, she had married John, a wonderfully kind schoolteacher she'd met at the school where they both taught. My son Patrick, now twenty-five, had a new job and couldn't take time off.

During the drive, I could already tell that the tranquility I'd experience in the week ahead would recharge me to help me to be present with what was about to happen in my life. I didn't yet know that my life would soon be divided into two distinct sections: before and after cancer.

The thirty-five-minute ferry ride officially signaled the beginning of my vacation. Standing on the ferry's open deck, I felt the gentle movement of the boat pulling away from the dock. Eventually, the lighthouse on land faded into the distance. I took a deep breath of the salty air and enjoyed my beloved onboard routine: I went inside and ordered a cup of clam chowder and an ice-cold beer.

About an hour later, we arrived at our salt box cottage in the town of Vineyard Haven. As soon as I unpacked, I began to dream of staying there forever. I slipped into a blissful mellowness.

During my week on the island, I walked the beach, collecting rocks and seashells, and listened to the voice of the ocean while watching the waves crash onto shore. The power of the ocean always made me ponder deep and wide ideas, like, what was my purpose here on earth? During my many walks, I tried to work through that universal question. I didn't settle on an answer, but I was grateful for the time and the peace to think about it.

I took long, tear-filled walks with Bruce and my kids. I rode a moped and ate fish and chips and fresh oysters at the Home Port restaurant. And lots of Mad Martha's local ice cream. I frequented my favorite shops, including Claudia's on Main Street in Edgartown where they always had the best locally made jewelry. There was Espresso Love and Mocha Motts, my favorite coffee spots, where I'd sit outside and people watch while sipping a hazelnut latte. I took pictures of sunsets and multi-colored hydrangeas. We all posed for family photos on the beach. I meditated often and wrote in my journal daily. After reflecting on my life, I discovered that I didn't have any regrets.

We shopped in Vineyard Haven, Oak Bluffs, and Edgartown. The owner of my favorite shop in Oak Bluffs overheard Sam telling me she wanted to buy me a necklace with the word *strength* engraved on it—as a reminder that I was strong and would make it through the cancer battle. At the register, the owner's eyes smiled at me through her gold wire rimmed glasses, and she said; "I want you to have this, no charge. I heard you talking. Please take it for good luck."

Samantha was only thirteen then. The sadness I sometimes saw in her eyes made me work to keep up a strong front whenever she was around. During one of our walks, I had wanted to share with her some words of wisdom, something a mother should want to convey about life, but I couldn't think of anything wise to say. I silently hoped that the parenting I'd done up to this point had been good enough. There was nothing more important to me than my children knowing that I never lost sight of what was important to me: my love for them. I couldn't bear that idea that they could ever experience anything like the kind of deep-seated loneliness and sense of being unloved that had plagued my childhood.

One afternoon I walked with Sarah down a gravel road that led to an oyster pond. I wanted to reach out to her and tell her that for most of my early life I'd felt like I'd been riding a bike with no training wheels, but at the same time I didn't want my child to see me feeling weak or defenseless. I wanted to share with her the unpredictability of my childhood—the fears, traumas, and loneliness. This cancer thing was starting to manifest closeted fears, and because I wasn't calling all the shots, I felt out of control, just as I'd felt growing up. I wanted her to know that I had never felt mothered, that back then I didn't even know what a good mother was. When she was growing up, my motherhood simply meant doing the opposite of everything my mother did. I kept almost all of this to myself, but I did share with Sarah my fear of dying. I wasn't ready to die, and Sarah reassured me that everything would be okay. I knew she was trying to be strong for me, and I truly appreciated that. When she reached out and hugged me, I welcomed it and rested my head on her shoulder, which soon became saturated with my tears.

I felt the safest during my many walks with Bruce. His unfailing love for me was an absolute gift in my life. I was deeply grateful that I didn't have to go through this alone. He was my sounding board. He kept a watch over my negative meter. His intelligence, strength, and positive attitude during this dark time made me love him even more.

One week later, dressed in a white hospital gown with blue snowflakes scattered across it, I sat upright on a stretcher in the pre-op holding area of UCONN Medical Center awaiting a sentinel node biopsy, followed by surgery—right lumpectomy with lymph node dissection.

The curtain to my left was closed, but I heard people on the other side laughing, which I found annoying. Laughing just seemed wrong when someone else is about to be wheeled into surgery. I wondered when I'd laugh like that again. My soft cotton, pale-blue, hospital-supplied socks with grippers on the bottom stuck out from the bottom of the white sheet. "Patrick loves these socks," I told Bruce. A few years back Patrick had had back surgery. When I stayed with him afterward to help out for a few days, he wore these socks nonstop, day and night. He continued to wear them for quite a while, long after he was feeling better. The memory of it made me smile.

Suddenly, my body started to shiver, and goose bumps appeared on my arms and legs. I didn't know if it was the cold in the room or just my nerves. The nurse brought me a warm, white blanket. I heard Bruce and my daughter Sarah whispering in the background, and it bothered me because I knew it was about me. "What are you guys talking about?" I asked. I was right; they were talking about me. They said they were making plans for after the surgery. Sarah was going to leave as soon as I went into surgery to meet Sam when she got off the school bus. I saw tears in Sarah's hazel eyes. She was playing with her shoulder-length brown hair—a nervous habit. It sounded like Bruce was sniffling.

I was filled with gratitude that Sarah had made the trip from Massachusetts where she lived with John and their two dogs. In just three months, she'd be turning twenty-eight. Where had all that time gone? She was my firstborn child, and her birth had changed my life, showing me for the first time in my life what unconditional love is. Her very presence soothed my soul.

While I waited to be wheeled into surgery, I wrote in my journal, which helped me remain distracted in this situation that had placed me so far out of my comfort zone and completely vulnerable. I was used to being a nurse. Today I was the patient. I wrote about the cancer. How my life was going along perfectly fine, and then—*boom, ba bang!*—the diagnosis! It was clear to me that my past was showing up in the present: the panic, the anxiety, the unpredictability, the rocking myself to sleep. All of it felt so familiar to me, and yet I'd thought I'd left it all behind, especially since meeting Bruce. But now the past was pushing its way forward again.

I wrote in my journal about other times in my life when I'd been confronted by hurdles, and that helped me to put my situation in perspective. This was just another hurdle I would overcome. This time I wasn't alone. My waiting time was up. A doctor from the radiology department arrived to take me to my first destination. He was dressed from head to toe in blue—a scrub top and pajama-like bottoms that tied at the waist. I noticed his wedding band tied into the strings that held up his pants. Bruce did the same thing with his ring when he was on call, and I considered whether this doctor had ever been on the other side. Had his wife or other loved one ever dealt with something like cancer? The matching light-blue mask hung low, like a sling on his neck. A sneaker top peaked out from the blue booties that covered his feet.

Bruce walked along the stretcher with me, and Sarah stayed behind. Together we ventured into the unknown.

First stop—nuclear medicine department for a sentinel node biopsy. This biopsy would determine how many lymph nodes, if any, were involved in my cancer. If any tested positive for cancer, they would also be removed during the surgery.

Next stop—radiology, where they took an X-ray to make sure the surgical clip—which resembled a small staple—was in the correct spot. I knew this part was important because it located and marked the area where the 1.6-centimeter tumor was.

Final destination—the operating room. With Bruce by my side, I was whisked down the hall. The stretcher stopped at the double doors that led into the operating room area. We kissed good-bye, and before my emotions had a chance to catch up with me, the pre-op relaxation drug hit my IV causing everything to go blurry.

Two hours later I woke up in the recovery room. I'd heard Bruce's voice. Everything went well, my doctor had removed all of the cancer cells she could see and then some. "We will wait to see if the margins are clear when the pathology report of the tissue comes back," she said. As far as the lymph nodes were concerned, she told us, "One lymph node was questionable, so I removed that. Otherwise, I don't think there is any lymph node involvement. The pathology report will tell us for sure."

With my chest wrapped like a mummy, I headed home to heal.

*I*t had been only two days since Marie was admitted into the hospital. My dad was on a bender, drinking round the clock. On the first day of Marie's absence, my dad kept asking me where she was. I played dumb and said I didn't know. That night, at one o'clock in the morning, my dad entered my bedroom drunk. "Where is your sister Marie?" he asked. "Your mother won't tell me where she is, and I *know* you know where she is. Tell me where!"

He looked at my Beatles *Abbey Road* poster, which hung scotch-taped over my bed. "You hippie," he said, ripping it off the wall and throwing it onto the floor. "You goddamn hippies," he said. When he said "hippies," I knew he was also referring to Marie. That drunken night, he ripped down everything I'd hung on my walls.

He swiped his hand across my desk and sent my schoolbooks and homework tumbling onto the floor. As he stomped towards my tall beige-colored dresser, I leaped out of bed, took a few steps towards him, and like an angry bear protecting its young roared, "Don't touch my stuff." My knees were shaking, but I held my ground. "Get out of my room."

My father ignored me, and my anger grew. I started breathing heavily and shouted, "Stop it! I hate you! Leave my room alone!" He still ignored me, moving on to fling all the belongings on my dresser onto the floor. My little jewelry box filled with earrings and the little treasures that sat atop it came crashing down. Everything I treasured was on the floor, including the silver cross necklace that my grandmother had given me for my birthday. I wanted to say something mean, to hurt him as he'd just hurt me. So, I said, "You're not going to be able to do this anymore, *real* soon."

He stared at me, and in a drunken garble shot back, "Whaddayou mean by that, Susan?"

Recognizing that I might have said too much, I said, "Nothing, I meant nothing, just leave my room." Hidden inside my dresser drawer were the bankbooks my mother had given me to hide for safekeeping.

My dad was now out of control. I didn't know at the time if he was using Marie's situation as an excuse to drink more or not. After many days of telling my mom, "You have to do something about Dad, he's out of control and bringing this whole family down with him," my mother confided in me her plan. She told me she had visited an attorney the day before, and he gave her a plan of action. The first step was to hide all the bankbooks. Done. Step two: obtain a restraining order against my father. Not done yet. Step three: ask for a separation. Not ready, not done yet. At least she was taking some action, I thought.

That time, my father's ranting and raving ended at about three in the morning, when he passed out. Then on the following night he was at it again. "If I can't sleep, nobody can sleep," he bellowed. He wanted to know where Marie was. Ceramic plates and glass breaking echoed from the kitchen. Slurring curse words, he walked around the house turning all of the lights on, including in my bedroom. Now we were all awake.

At one o'clock in the morning, my mom told us to get into the car because we would be leaving. We drove to my grandmother's house thirty minutes away and slept there for the night. Before we left the house, my mother told my father where Marie was. He was furious.

The next day, we were back home, and that evening, after I'd just wrapped myself up in a warm fleece blanket and gotten cozy on the sofa to watch one my favorite TV shows, I heard voices coming from outside. Looking out the front window, I saw my sister Marie getting out of an ambulance. My mind raced. *Oh my God, what is she doing home? Holy Shit! What am I going to do?* She was supposed to be in the hospital, so I didn't understand why an ambulance had just brought her home. She was walking quickly towards the back door, and her arms swung by her sides like pendulums on a clock that had gone haywire. She was jacketless, shoeless, and wore blue hospital bootie socks on her feet. Her clothes were a wrinkled mess.

She came into the house and started clanging things in the kitchen. Her voice was deep and belligerent. She spoke of the FBI, of being spied on, and of others hurting her. She spoke of conspiracies and a plot to kill her. Her deep voice scared me because it sounded like an evil spirit possessed her. She blurted, "I will kill you if you get any closer."

Terrified, I ran down the hall to my parent's bedroom and locked the door behind me. I thought, *Holy shit! What am I going to do?* The last time I saw Marie she wasn't moving—she was catatonic. Now, she had a chilling look and sound to her. Without having to look up the phone number, I dialed the numbers on the fancy antique European phone in my parent's bedroom and asked for the labor and delivery unit. "Can I please speak to Joan McNally? It's an emergency." My mom answered. In a frantic voice I said, "Mom! Marie is home, and she's scaring me!"

"What do you mean Marie is home?"

"She arrived home by ambulance just a couple of minutes ago," I answered.

"Oh my God, she shouldn't be out of the hospital," my mother said in a panicky voice that I'd never heard before. "Shit. That bastard, he must have gone and taken her out." I figured she was referring to my dad.

"What do you want me to do, Mom? She's saying scary things."

She was as shocked as I was that my sister was home and told me she'd leave work and would be home as quickly as possible. She said, "In the meantime, try to stay away from her."

I was frantic. Praying that my other sisters or brother wouldn't come home yet, I'd hidden scrunched down, arms wrapped around my trembling knees on the side of my parents' bed, hardly breathing just in case Marie came into the room. *What will she do if she finds me? What if she sees me and tries to kill me? Hail Mary full of grace . . .*

In the kitchen, Marie started speaking in a language I didn't recognize. There were two voices talking to each other, and neither one of them sounded like Marie. I thought for sure I'd be dead if she found me.

The clanging of pots and pans rang throughout the house. Then, in a hostile voice, she shrieked something about knives. My head perked up from my knees when I heard that.

Although I hadn't seen *The Exorcist*, I'd seen a preview, and Marie sounded like the possessed Linda Blair in the film. *Why is she talking in such a low, deep tone? Is she possessed by the devil?*

Later, I found out that my father had gone to the hospital that day and signed Marie out against medical advice.

My mom arrived home about forty-five minutes later with the police. My grandmother, her mother, showed up shortly after. They held hands as paramedics walked Marie to the ambulance. My dad wasn't home when the ambulance took her away wrapped in a white straitjacket. She was readmitted to the local psychiatric hospital even though her care was going to involve more than the local psychiatric hospital could handle.

The following day, my mother went to the Springfield Courthouse and obtained an emergency involuntary commitment order for Marie. She told me that Marie was going to be admitted to Northampton State Hospital for the criminally insane. She continued to talk, but though I saw her lips move, I couldn't hear what she was saying. I'd gone somewhere else in my mind.

A massive dark cloud continued to churn over 60 Nottingham Street. A storm was brewing, and I didn't want to be around when it hit.

*T*welve days post-surgery, my birthday arrived with no big fan-fare, unlike the previous year when I'd been surprised with a fiftieth birthday party. The townhouse was empty, and all our belongings sat on a moving truck headed for St. Louis. I'd placed the last of my personal belongings in my blue tote bag and walked to the car. It was official, we were moving to the Midwest. Even though I was excited and had been preparing for this move for some time, the ominous cloud of cancer overshadowed my elation.

Bruce, Samantha, and I piled into Bruce's SUV. It was filled to the brim for our big road trip: suitcases, household items, personal belongings, a small dog cage for Molly, a kitten cage for Gracie, and a cage for Hammy the hamster. Snacks and drinks sat in a bag on the floor of the backseat where Samantha settled in. Her portable DVD player was already fired up. In my tote bag were plenty of reading materials to last me the entire sixteen-hour trip: magazines, catalogs, a book, and the "All You Need to Know about Chemotherapy" booklet that I had picked up during my last visit with my oncologist.

This was the longest road trip I'd ever taken: eleven hundred miles from Farmington, Connecticut, to St. Louis. Bruce had seen the Midwest before, but when I went to sign all the paperwork for the purchase of the house, I had seen only some of what Missouri was like. Samantha had grown up on the East Coast and had no sense of any of the Midwest. We were thrilled when we drove past the signs welcoming us to all the states between Connecticut and Missouri, but when I read the sign that said, "Welcome to Missouri," I felt lonely. It had finally hit me that this was my new home. My new reality was that my family and friends were very far away. I'd left my support system over a thousand miles away, and now I found myself pondering how I'd get through all the changes that were concurrently happening in my life. Had we made the wrong choice? I was going through a bad stretch of life, and even with my husband and child by my side I felt alone.

We drove through St. Louis and twenty minutes later reached our new town of Wildwood. The entrance to Woodcliff Heights was decorated with pretty pink, white, and yellow annuals that I hadn't noticed on my earlier visit with Mary.

We pulled our car into the driveway. The SOLD sign with its big bold letters still sat out front. The three of us walked up the sidewalk toward the front door of the house, which Bruce and Samantha were seeing for the first time. Bruce pushed open the door while Samantha and I turned around and took in the neighborhood. We walked around the yard and admired the newness of our Tudor-style brick home. We could smell the freshness of the mulch from the recently landscaped front yard. A pink flowering tree and three miniature red rose bushes in full bloom flourished to the right of the house. This was the largest house I'd ever lived in, and I felt reassured by its positive energy, inside and out. It boggled my mind that our house had five bathrooms. I'd grown up in a home with nine people who shared a single bathroom. This size house for a family of three seemed excessive to me, but I knew that Bruce felt proud to be able afford a home like this.

Bruce popped his head out of the doorframe and called out to me, "C'mon Sue, I wanna carry you over the threshold." I smiled and walked toward him. Samantha looked on as he scooped me up and carried me like a new bride through the front door. "Welcome to our new home," he said. After he put me down on the other side, Saman-tha said, "My turn." She giggled as Bruce carried her into the house. The minute he released her from his arms, she bolted upstairs to check out her new bedroom. I was deeply thankful for Samantha's positive attitude about the move. This was a big change for her, and Bruce and I promised her that we would live in this house at least until she graduated from high school. She was comforted by that and embraced the new adventure.

The next morning, the moving truck arrived carrying our life's belongings, and we spent all of Sunday unpacking boxes and deciding where everything should go. I was so busy unpacking and admiring our new home that several times I forgot I had breast cancer.

I thought about the rest of my family—my older kids, my mom, sisters, and brother who lived in Massachusetts. They were all miles and miles away now, and the thought of that distance brought with it more feelings of isolation and fear. But I shut the door on those thoughts, hoping they'd simply go away.

PRIOR TO OUR move, Bruce had phoned Jim Barrett, one of the partners in the MFM group Bruce was joining, to tell him the news about my breast cancer. Jim told Bruce he would understand com-pletely if we wanted to delay the move, but we decided against it. There were too many things already in motion. Contracts had been signed for the practice, the old house, the new house, and I was committed to not let cancer make any decisions for me. I was already angry that my diagnosis had gotten in the way of my excitement about this new chapter in my life. I usually enjoyed change. I'd always thought it was the only path to growth; accept change, go with it, see where it leads. One of my favorite sayings is, "Change is the only con-stant in life." In my professional life, I liked challenge, and I'd felt ready for change about every five years. If I wasn't learning and developing new skills, I wanted to move on. This quality had served me well, and I'd moved up rung after rung on the nursing ladder into bigger and better jobs. Now cancer was introducing a new look at the idea of change, but I was determined to stay strong and in control whenever possible.

After a busy day of unpacking, I lay in bed thinking about my upcoming appointment the following day with my new oncologist. If he didn't agree with Dr. Ayers, which doctor should I trust? What were my other options if I didn't like this new doctor?

I met Dr. Nettles the following morning in the newly built cancer center, and my first impression was that he was full of himself. While I sat on the examining table and Bruce sat in the chair, we briefly discussed my diagnosis and my medical records from UConn Medical Center.

I sat there waiting to discuss my treatment options when Dr. Nettle's focus turned to Bruce. He asked him about his new practice and what had brought him to St. Louis. I was beyond irritated by their small talk as they discussed themselves and their medical practices. I was tempted to say, "Hello, patient over here!" but I kept my mouth shut. Once more it seemed to be all about Bruce's job, which left me feeling alone again. After the appointment, I was at least comforted that Dr. Nettles's proposed plan for me was identical to Dr. Ayers's.

The following week was filled with meetings and a slew of tests and procedures. Port-a-cath placement, CT scans, chest X-rays, PET scan, blood work, MRI, and bone scans.

Along with all my medical appointments, I was grateful that I kept busy with all that came along with moving into a new home. However, the initial loneliness I'd felt wasn't going away.

My lack of control over my situation brought back several familiar childhood feelings: loss, anger, abandonment, and fear about what would happen next—like a fleet of submarines, they surfaced. I started having nightmares of being trapped in buildings, always with no way out, and dying before anyone could find me. Anxiety and sadness loomed over me.

In the second week of August, I had the port-a-cath placed. After the surgical procedure, I was in a lot of pain. Already I hated having a foreign object inside my body. It was supposed to make my chemo treatment easier so that blood draws would be seamless. It promised less bruising as well. The port-a-cath made access to the vein easy, so I reluctantly accepted the pain. Over time, I'd come to feel grateful, but I wasn't there yet. Bruce was able to be with me for the procedure, but then he announced that he wouldn't be with me for those that would follow. The new practice was relying on him to jump right in, and he would be seeing patients the following week. I wanted and needed Bruce to be the rock I was used to. I needed him with me. That he turned toward the direction of his career set off more feelings of abandonment.

It was a warm, sunny September day in St. Louis, yet I was chilled to the bone as I arrived at the David C. Pratt Cancer Center at my scheduled time of eleven o'clock. Friday was "chemo day," scheduled to fall right before the weekend so that Bruce would be home with me on the Saturdays and Sundays following treatment. I used to love Fridays, knowing that the weekend came right after. Weekends brought endless possibilities. Now Fridays had taken on a whole different meaning. For the next three months, every third Friday was chemo day. I called it "hell week times four." I'd always imagined hell to be a place of great suffering, but this level of suffering was worse than I'd imagined. For me, it was a plunge into a world of darkness. I never felt I had much choice about chemo; it was supposed to increase my long-term survival rate, so of course I opted in.

The David C. Pratt Cancer Center was adjacent to St. John's Mercy Medical Center, where Bruce now worked. As one of the largest hospitals in the area, its parking lot was always full. I'd asked Sarah to drive me to my first appointment because driving yourself to a chemotherapy session is just wrong. It would be like transporting yourself to a torture chamber. I was grateful to have my daughter helping me, but it was clear to my heart that she was just filling in for my unavailable husband. I had learned early on in life to not have any expectations. Keeping my feelings to myself, sometimes not even acknowledging them, was an effective defense mechanism. The shield of armor that I had built up over time blocked me from asking for help. I'd gone so long not asking for what I needed that I turned off my needs. Even though Bruce arranged for someone to be with me for each session, he was my husband, and I felt he should have been there. If the situation had been reversed, there would be nothing more important to me than being there for him.

My name was called, and Sarah (who had flown in the day before) followed me into the "chemo room." The sun was shining brightly through a large wall of windows, beneath which sat six beige leather recliners. An additional two recliners sat on the other side of the room. The nurse greeted us and told me to pick an empty chair. "Chairs one, two, three, or four are available," she said, motioning in the direction of the line-up. Seats five and six were already occupied, as were the two across the room. I felt like I was on *The Price is Right* and said, "I choose chair number three." I sat down on the beige recliner and placed my laptop and reading material on the side table. Sarah handed me my favorite fuzzy blanket, and I put it over my lap. Then, like the new kid in class, I glanced over to see my cohorts. There was a woman to my left who looked about my age. She wore a tall, colorful turban. I've never liked turbans and was determined that I wasn't going to wear one once I lost my hair. There was a woman seated in the recliner and a man, most likely her husband, sat beside her. They were each reading novels. Seeing their togetherness made me miss Bruce even more. Two other people sat on the other side of the silent room with their eyes closed. Nobody looked up to greet me.

There were silver and black headphones and a small television in my little cubby area. I turned on the TV, put the headphones on, and started channel-hopping. I stopped when I found *The Ellen De-Generes Show.* I giggled when she began her monologue and became immediately self-conscious. Nobody was laughing in here.

I sat upright, quiet and complacent as the poison entered my body. Drip by drip. Right away, I wanted to pull out the IV and make a run for it. But I was defenseless and saw no alternative. I waited for the attack to occur and hoped that my body could defend itself against this poison.

The chemo treatment started as an odd tingling in my head. I felt the poison right away. It was potent and engulfed my entire being. A sudden strong cosmic rush shot through my head, making a bull's-eye landing in my brain. My ears rang like church bells. I lost my hearing. I imagined the drug attacking my brain cells, killing each one that it came across. Heat like a raging inferno engulfed me from the inside out. My face flushed as if I'd been badly sunburned. My entire body went limp, down to my toes. I imagined that I might have looked as if I were sleeping comfortably with my eyes closed, but I was anything but comfortable. I was scared because I'd never felt anything like this before, and there was no turning back. I was alone in my thoughts, so I prayed: *Please, God, make me strong and brave so that I can get through this. Please do not let this poison ruin me forever. Please, please, please let there be no medical errors that cause me to lose my precious life.*

I reclined the chair, turned onto my right side, and curled up into a fetal position. Sarah asked, "Mom, are you okay?" I couldn't possibly share with her how I truly felt because I didn't even know myself. I just nodded my heavy, woozy, chemo-soaked head. If my brain had been a sponge, it would have been dripping wet. If I was scared, she would have been infinitely more scared for me. I did what I was good at when I was scared: I switched into survival mode. I went somewhere else in my mind. I'd read Elisabeth Kübler-Ross's book *On Death and Dying* and realized this is what was called denial. I focused on trying to relax and eventually fell into a merciful sleep that, just for a while, allowed me to escape the utter awfulness of it all.

Five hours later, no longer a chemo virgin, I was more than ready to go home. Feeling dizzy, weak, and as if I'd just drunk an entire bottle of champagne, I stood up and leaned into Sarah. My brain felt lost in a dense fog.

On the car ride home, I attempted to form a sentence about how I was feeling, but my brain didn't cooperate. I had no idea why I couldn't articulate words. During the thirty-minute drive I attempted conversation a few more times, but I simply couldn't make words flow from my mind to my mouth. "Don't worry, Mom," Sarah assured me. "It's okay." I believed her and rested my head back on the seat and dozed off.

Later that day, nausea, hiccups, and indigestion came on in an angry storm.

There are stages of grief that accompany a cancer diagnosis—denial, anger, bargaining, depression, and acceptance—and I flipped and flopped through all of them in no particular order. I remained convinced that each stage was magnified by the fact that I was a stranger in a strange town. My people weren't within reach, and I still had three more rounds of poison to ingest.

CHAPTER 8

1972–1974

*A*fter Marie was confined to Northampton State Hospital in early November it was as if someone put an accelerant in my dad's beer. He went from drinking heavily only on the weekends to drinking very heavily every night. His drinking always started off with a tall glass of beer, but after about three beers, he'd start drinking right from the bottle. After beer number five or six, his rage surfaced and violence followed. My parents' relationship was in a downward spiral and spinning fast. They barely spoke to each other anymore, and when they did talk, it always blew into an argument, usually about Marie.

I'd wake up many mornings to find the kitchen trashed, the floor covered with broken plates and glasses strewn about. Empty beer bottles perched haphazardly along the Formica countertop. The portable black-and-white television on the kitchen table ran white snow. The lights on the first floor still on. Sometimes Dad would even be passed out at the kitchen table.

I desperately wanted my old dad back—the one who was fun to be around. The one who whistled while doing chores around the house, and who often asked one of us to run and get him a screwdriver or other tool he needed. He taught us the difference between a flat and Phillips-head screwdriver, between a wrench and pliers. He loved basketball and taught us all how to shoot "nothing but net" baskets. His favorite game was "egg," in which one person shoots the basketball, and if they make the shot, the next person has to make the same exact shot; if that second shooter misses, they earn themselves a letter until spelling "egg" means you're out. The last person standing wins.

The dad I knew then was tall, dark-haired, and handsome. He was a sharp dresser and a good athlete. He wore Sperry boat shoes with no socks, plaid shorts, khakis, and cardigan sweaters. For work, he'd wear a suit and tie, brown wing-tipped shoes, and a fedora hat. He never wore sneakers or jeans. He was easy to talk to back then, and everyone who knew him called him Bob. When I was four years old, he earned a law degree from American International College in Springfield, Massachusetts, while working full time at the Travelers Insurance Company. In the early days he was our hero.

When I was eight, nine, and ten years old, our Christmases were the best ever. I thought the Christmas catalog from Sears was actually from Santa's workshop. Every year I waited anxiously for the thick catalog to appear in the mail, and when it arrived, Dad told us, "You can pick three things and ask Santa for them." Again and again, that catalog was passed from one kid to the other, ending up tattered and frayed by the time Christmas arrived. And every year, we received the toys we asked for. The feeling I had on Christmas morning was one I wished I could hold onto forever.

By the time I was a teenager, those beautiful days were gone, replaced by a life-sucking enemy that deadened the pulse of our family. A constant unmitigated chaos began to reign in our house, making it unbearable to be home for any length of time, especially on the weekends when my mother was working. When she wasn't working, she was aloof and walked around like a deer in headlights. If you hung around our house for long, you'd probably be the next target of my father's rage.

If my family had been a ship, we would have been the *Titanic*, sinking rapidly as water poured in from all sides.

When he wasn't drinking or drunk, I loved my father dearly. But by the time I was fifteen, the man I'd grown up with barely existed anymore. He used to be so handsome, dressed in his business suit and tie, smelling of Old Spice. Now he smelled of body odor and beer and wore the same stained brown corduroy trousers, white Oxford shirt, and ratty orange sweater for days. Then he started skipping work.

I wondered why Dad was now home during the workweek and not at his job. When I asked Mom, she told me that he'd been fired. He told her that it was due to missing too many days of work.

My father's favorite pastime had always been catalog shopping from Sears, and his new unemployment left him all kinds of time to peruse the pages he so loved. It wasn't uncommon to open the door to our glass-enclosed back porch and see it stacked with boxes. One year he even bought an entire above ground pool from Sears and put it together himself. Then one day during my freshman year, I came home from school to find several bright red-and-silver machines on our side porch. I hadn't had the slightest clue what they were or where they had come from, but I knew it wasn't Sears. I walked out to the driveway and peeked into my dad's car. It was filled to the brim with coin-operated peanut dispenser machines, the same kinds of machine I saw on the side porch. His car seats were littered with packages of pantyhose and plastic bottles filled with coins. Quarters, dimes, and nickels sat in clear plastic containers on the passenger seat. Yellow legal pads were scattered around. The windows were dirty, and his favorite orange cardigan was stained and hanging on the back of the driver's seat. Empty beer cans, Chesterfield King cigarette butts, and wrappers were strewn about the floor.

He had bought a vending machine business, and his job was now selling peanuts and pantyhose. He had simply declared to my mother, "I need a job, and this will keep me busy." My mother's reply was, "Bob, I think you've lost your mind."

So rather than defend the innocent in courtrooms, my father spent his days hanging out in bars, drinking beer, and trying to sell peanuts.

Mom had told me that my dad worked extremely hard to become a lawyer. He went to night school part-time for five years, so I didn't understand why he'd just give up his career.

The same blue station wagon that we'd used for family trips to Cape Cod just two years earlier was now filled to the brim with carnival junk and pantyhose. It made no sense to me that he seemed so unphased to go from being a lawyer to a peanut-vending-machine owner. When I asked him why he lost his job, all he said was, "Well, I'm doing this now."

To be witness to my sister's mental breakdown and then my father's fall from grace was surreal. Was he, too, having a breakdown? It seemed clear to me that the part of my dad's brain that involved rational thinking was now drenched with alcohol. I was humiliated for him and our family and felt as if we were all living in one long nightmare. I was so young, and yet I'd already known so very much suffering.

Then the reality of the situation crashed down on my psyche: if Marie had lost her mind and my mom was on the edge of a nervous breakdown, who was going to be in charge? *Oh my God, is there a panic button somewhere? Because I need to press it. What's going to happen now?*

The Christmas holidays were approaching, and I was really not looking forward to them. That Christmas Eve, my dad put the record player on the kitchen table and sang along with one of his favorite Christmas albums, cross-eyed drunk. It was only my siblings and grandparents who witnessed this show, but I was still embarrassed. I left the room in disgust and escaped to my bedroom. Christmas just wasn't the same without Marie at home. The Christmas tree, sparsely decorated with ornaments and silver tinsel, sat in the corner of the living room looking pathetic, just like our lives, just like my home. And this year the tree skirt was clearly visible because there were so few presents to cover it.

Hoping to understand what was going on with my father, my mother started attending Al-Anon meetings. She even asked me to go with her, but I refused. At fifteen years old, I didn't want to sit there and feel the shame ooze out of my pores. I really didn't want to understand what my dad was doing or why. All I knew was that he was out of control—quickly descending down into this deep dark hole, and I wanted to be nowhere near it.

At this point, my mother appeared to be running on empty. Afraid that she would break down at any moment, I took on even more of a mothering role. I'm sure I thought that, with Marie already sent away, if my mother also lost her mind, I'd become the woman of the house anyway, especially to my younger siblings. Mary and Margaret loved when I'd tell them bedtime stories about places that they could only dream of. I wanted them to think of anywhere but here and to fall asleep dreaming about how wonderful life could be. I realized that caring for them was the only time I felt a real sense of worth. I became good at it. Taking care of them also took my mind off the nightmare we were all stuck in.

The beginning of the new year held a somber tone. Because she didn't want to be alone, my mom asked me to go to court with her, and I agreed. I felt sorry for her. I also wanted to make sure she followed through on getting a restraining order. It was time. It was long past time.

The courtroom was scattered with lawyers and their clients. Most were sitting on pew-like benches waiting for their turn in front of the judge. My mom and I sat in silence on a dark mahogany bench toward the front of the courtroom. I looked around the room and saw my dad's law partner sitting off to the side. The judge entered the room, everyone stood up, and court was called to order. My insides trembled when my mom's name was called. She must have lost at least fifteen pounds in the past six months. Her five-foot-two-inch frame looked fragile, and her blue flowered dress drooped on her. She held a tissue in her right hand, and her voice quivered as she stated her case. My embarrassment prevented me from looking anywhere but at the floor. The judge and the fifteen or so other people in the courtroom that day now officially knew our dirty family secret: my father was a drunk.

Sitting high behind a deep mahogany bench, the judge agreed to a legal separation and a restraining order, and he ordered my dad to complete a thirty-day alcohol rehab program. To my mother he said, "It's a shame, Bob is such a great guy. Let's hope he gets better."

This was my father's territory. The judge knew him, and so did my mom's lawyer. My dad's law partner walked over to my mom, and as if she were at a funeral, shook her hand and said that he was sorry about what was happening. A few other people stopped and spoke briefly with my mother, and it was clear that they all really liked my father and were pulling for him. I wished he could have seen all these expressions of genuine concern and care.

Standing outside on the steps of the courthouse, I felt myself let out a big sigh. I thought I could almost see a light at the end of a tunnel, I hoped it wasn't a train.

By this time my dad hadn't been home in a few days, and nobody seemed to know where he was. When he showed up the next day looking contrite, my mom approached him in the driveway and said, "Bob you can't come in the house. I left your things out in the garage." Then she told him about the court order. Before she turned her back on him and went back inside the back door, she added, "I had no choice. I had to do it for the children—you have to get better."

He was to turn himself in to his attorney by tomorrow. He said, "You're out of your mind."

He said he wanted to talk to me, so I went out to the garage where he was packing up the blue station wagon. "Susan, why did you go to court with your mother?" he asked me. I didn't know how he had found out that I had gone.

"Because she asked me to. She didn't want to go alone," I replied.

"You disgraced me in front of all of my colleagues," he said. "You embarrassed me, Susan. There is nothing the matter with me." He felt betrayed, thought I'd dishonored his name in court. I'd told him I had just sat there on the dark mahogany bench in silence, but he didn't believe me. I hadn't done anything wrong and still he made me feel ashamed.

"Dad, you have a real drinking problem and you need help," I said.

"I don't have a drinking problem. I don't drink any of that hard stuff, only beer," he replied.

He finished packing the car and picked up the basketball that lay on the driveway and twirled it around like a top. Then he dribbled and took a shot. He missed. I sighed, "It doesn't matter, Dad, you need help, and so does Marie." Nobody was talking about Marie and her situation. Nobody was sticking up for her. Somebody needed to speak up—somebody needed to say *something*. Just one year earlier she'd had a normal life, and now she was in a mental institution. I just couldn't wrap my brain around that. "You need to let her stay where she is to continue get the help she needs. You can't just go there and take her out," I said. "And . . . you need to get help too." He ignored me again.

He shot a few more hoops before rolling the ball into the garage. "You don't know what you're talking about," he said as he got into his car.

By then I'd grown very tired of being the only one who ever spoke truth in my family. Nobody else seemed to care. It was as if everyone else had given up.

After that day, my father didn't speak to me again for years. But before he drove away, he threw in one more jab; he asked me if the rumor going around about Sheila, my twin sister was true. "I don't know what you're talking about," I lied.

CHAPTER 9

FALL 2007

*A*s a result of the chemo drug I was on, the oncology nurse told me that I'd probably start to lose my hair within two weeks. I wondered if I'd have the guts to watch my hair fall out, or if I'd shave it off myself. What was I going to look like bald? It had been just a few days since my first chemo treatment. My daughters, my mother, and my husband thought the proactive approach to this hair loss thing was the best option. "Shave it," they said.

My mind hadn't yet caught up to all that was happening. I wanted this speeding train to stop for a bit, or at least slow down so I could catch my breath. I was still in denial that I actually had cancer. I'd had short hair before but had been growing it out for a few years and was pretty excited that it was now shoulder length. In addition to loving my new length, a bald head on a woman screams "cancer patient." People had always told me I had nice hair. I didn't want to be hairless. People would stare at me, feel sorry for me. Children would be scared of me. I wasn't ready to look like a cancer patient. Cancer and I just didn't belong in the same sentence. Wasn't this one of those things that happened to *other* people?

Shaving my hair before it fell out seemed like a good idea to me too, eventually, but I just wasn't ready yet. I didn't know why I couldn't make the decision. Passivity drove me crazy. It defined my childhood; back then, something was done only if the shit hit the fan and there was no other choice left. But now, in the frightening and unpredictable environment that had become my life, I needed to feel I had some degree of control. My sanity depended on it.

It was a Sunday night. Sarah was going back home to Massachusetts the following day, and she wanted to be here for the shaving. In fact, she wanted to do most of it. Even though I wanted to bow out of the whole situation, I realized that waiting for the inevitable would be much worse. That would have given the cancer all the control. My mother had just arrived from Massachusetts to be with me for my second round of chemo and also encouraged the option that would likely make me feel most in control. So, I agreed to shave my head, knowing that everything about it would be awful.

I put on the Winnie the Pooh T-shirt my kids had bought me years earlier. I loved that T-shirt. It was usually reserved for bedtime because there was just something about it that always comforted me. Bruce pulled the shaver from the cabinet and placed it on the counter. In a moment of lightheartedness, I said to him, "That's not the same shaver you use on the dog, is it?"

He looked at me with raised brows and a sneaky expression that seemed to be mixed with empathy, and he said, "Yep, it actually is."

With a whisp of sarcasm, I said, "Okay, now my dignity is definitely at an all-time low."

Sarah asked if she could be the one to start the shaving. Bruce, Samantha, and my mom all agreed. In the second that the buzzing began, I felt invisible—like a child all over again. Here I was, fifty years old, and what I wanted more than anything was to hold my childhood doll.

THE FIRST TIME I saw Little Miss No Name she was on a Christmas television commercial in 1965, I immediately felt a strong connection to her. I was eight years old, and she was more than a doll. She touched my soul and at the time was a metaphor for my life.

My two sisters and I had just finished our hot chocolates topped with marshmallow fluff. My mom always made these for us after we'd had a busy afternoon playing in the snow. I loved the way the marshmallow took on a frothy texture as it melted.

We drank our hot chocolates in the cellar where we sat in front of the large brown gas heater to defrost our nearly frostbitten feet. My dad had turned this area of the basement into the "kids' space." A week earlier, he'd come down to see how we liked the new area and greeted us by saying, "Hi, boys," which he liked to say because it always got a rise out of us. Looking back, I think he liked to tease us because he didn't know what else to do with six daughters.

"Dad, we are not boys!" we'd protest, but secretly I loved the attention. I was starving, and I devoured any attention from my parents.

The basement floor was made of cream-colored square tiles, and a multi-colored rag rug covered the area directly in front of the heater. There was a twenty-inch black-and-white TV set, and a couple of tag-sale chairs sat in front of it. This was where all we kids spent most of our time. In the winter, we bundled ourselves into a large, dark-green fleece blanket, lay on our stomachs, and watched TV while the warm air from the heater blew on our feet. I knew when my feet started to itch that the blood was coming back into my toes. Our mittens and socks, still stiff with snow, sat on top of the heater.

We were watching *Casper the Friendly Ghost* when a commercial came on for "Little Miss No Name." I immediately declared, "I want her for Christmas!"

My twin, Sheila, said, "Why would you want a doll like that? She's ugly." I didn't think she was ugly—quite the opposite, actually. Her lips turned downward into a frown, but I loved that. It made her seem more real to me. She had colossal sad brown eyes, like mine. Her hair was a dirty blond color, a crystalline teardrop glistened from her left cheek, and her one hand reached out like she was asking for a coin. She wore a ragged dress made of burlap with stitched-on pockets, held together in the back with a large safety pin.

When I saw her for the first time, it was as if my own reflection looked back at me. I had cute dresses, it was true, not like her ragged dress. Yet, I identified with her. I didn't see her begging for money; I saw her begging for love. I didn't see her sadness; I saw that she needed love and care. She looked like I felt. I didn't tell anyone about my feelings of loneliness, but I told Little Miss No Name everything.

I was ecstatic on Christmas morning to find her among my presents, and I cared for her as if she were my child. I covered up her bare legs under my blanket at nighttime, caressed her teardrop, and kept her warm and cozy while the two of us rocked ourselves to sleep. I gave her the attention that I so desperately craved. While my mother cared for my new twin baby sisters, I directed my love toward my doll.

BACK IN THE bathroom, with the buzzing sound of the shaver in my ear, I still felt the need to hold onto something. Sarah stopped shaving long enough for me to pick up my dog, Molly, who had been at my feet. I placed her on my lap and held on tight.

Sarah and Samantha thought it would be fun to shave my hair in a Mohawk style first. But I wasn't in the mood for joking around.

"Come on," I said to them, "let's just get this freaking thing over with." I sat on the stool in my bathroom that faced the large ceiling-to-counter mirror that covered the entire sink and vanity area. My mom, Sarah, Samantha, and Bruce stood around me in a semicircle. I wept as my wavy dark black hair dropped to the floor all around me. When Sarah finished shaving the back of my head, I reached around and felt my exposed neck. Cancer suddenly became real to me. There was no turning back now. My neck felt prickly and cold, and I couldn't stop crying. Sarah and Samantha both wrapped their arms around my shoulders and buried their heads into my neck. "It's ok, Mom, you're going to look beautiful," they both said.

Sarah turned me around on the stool and then Bruce, my mom, and, Samantha each took a turn shaving my scalp a bit, completing the sides and front. After they were all finished, I turned my head side to side in the mirror, checking out my new baldness. I shuddered at the reflection looking back at me. Even though I hated my new look, I took a deep breath of relief—it was finally over, and there were no weird bumps or marks on my scalp.

My mother had tears in her eyes. Bruce had a colossal smile on his face and said, "You look beautiful" as he hugged me.

I'd just been now stripped of another part of what made me feel like a woman. First there was the lumpectomy, which took out a quarter of my breast, then the chemo that killed not only the cancer cells but left few of my healthy ones. Now my beautiful, dark hair was gone. As I looked in the mirror and rubbed the top of my head, I wondered if I'd ever look like myself again.

After it was all done, I changed out of my Winnie the Pooh T-shirt and into my pajamas, curled up in my bed, pulled the covers over my head, and fell asleep.

A few weeks after the shaving event, Bruce received a call from California, where his mother lived. My mother-in-law, Joy, had been sick with pulmonary fibrosis but had been doing pretty well. We'd talked about her moving closer to us, after we had settled into St. Louis. She had liked the idea, especially because Samantha was her only grandchild, and she lit up whenever Samantha was around. She had a caregiver who checked on her daily and took her places that she needed to go. A portable oxygen tank helped on most days with her breathing. Now her caregiver, Heidi, was calling to say that Joy had been using the oxygen more and more but was still having difficulty breathing. Her condition was rapidly deteriorating. Eventually a hospice nurse would be called in.

Concerned with his mother's deteriorating health, Bruce booked a flight to California for him and Samantha. I was disappointed that I couldn't go with them, but I was in no condition to fly across the country. My second round of chemo was less than a week away.

Bruce called me with an update when he arrived at his mother's house. He was surprised by how frail Joy looked. She was comfortable though, not anxious, and resting in bed. Bruce and Samantha were taking turns lying with her, each saying their good-byes.

My emotions were pulled in different directions. Would I have to say good-bye forever to my dear mother-in-law over the phone? I was sad for Bruce and tried to feel compassion for his situation, but I was dealing with my own battle for my life and felt helpless and alone. I already knew Bruce couldn't be here for my second round of chemo, but now he wasn't even going to be with me for the days after, which were always the worst. I understood the situation, but I still felt upset by it. Upset that it was happening and upset that I had no control.

With a heavy heart, I spoke with Joy by phone and told her how much I loved her and that I'd miss her. I thanked her for raising such a wonderful man. I told her how important she was to me, how I would miss our conversations, how much I loved the fact that she treated me like a daughter, and how very sad I was that I couldn't be there with her. When I stopped sobbing, she said. "Sue, I love you, and I know Bruce is in good hands." And with that, we said our good-byes.

Joy's death triggered past feelings of grief and loss for me. I thought of my childhood, and the recent loss of my home, friends, and family. I yearned for my sisters' laughter, the company of my friends, and the comfy-cozy feeling I'd created in my last home. Everything was different here in my new home. I still didn't have a kitchen table, and parts of the house echoed because most of the rooms were still bare. The emptiness in my home matched the hollow feeling inside me.

That same night, my mom told me that she wanted to stay with me a bit longer so I wouldn't be alone while Bruce and Samantha were away. She ended up staying for three months, the entire duration of my chemo treatments. Without asking, she took over, taking care of all the tasks and responsibilities I wasn't able to handle. She made sure Samantha had what she needed for school, watched her get on and off the bus, and even watched Samantha's two favorite television shows with her, *Gossip Girl* and *Seventh Heaven*. She was my voice when I needed her to be. She'd sit with Samantha and ask her if she was ok and encouraged her to share her feelings about her mom having cancer. I think my mother felt a camaraderie with Samantha because she'd been around Samantha's age when her own mother had breast cancer. My mom shared with me that she tried to offer Samantha the kinds of interactions she'd wanted when her own mother had been ill: comforting, conversation, and making a lot of brownies. The end result of all of this would be that Samantha and my Mom became very close.

This was the first time in my life that I'd felt unconditional love from my mother. It was awkward at first, having her at my home and taking over my duties. I had avoided her for most of my thirties as week after week the anger I felt for her spilled all over my therapist's floor.

All through my 30s and 40s, whenever I'd finish a visit with my mother, I'd be left with a sadness that would take days to shake, so I kept my distance. I had no interest in using those visits to try to make up for lost time by having talks, and I also didn't want to be made to feel guilty about being a bad daughter all those years that I'd essentially stayed away. Forgetting the pain of the past was simply easier when she wasn't around. So for decades, I didn't know what it was like to have a mother's care, to have my needs met by a parent; for this reason alone, my cancer turned out to be a special gift, a second chance at love and acceptance. I had to learn how to be a daughter again, and I allowed myself to savor every bit of her caring attention. I was finally being given what I had craved so desperately as a child.

I started feeling better the following week, except for my puffy hands and feet and the constant heartburn. When Bruce and Samantha returned from California, they were both emotionally exhausted, but the next day, Bruce threw himself right back into work. I'd hoped he could have taken some time off to be with me. I wasn't dying, but in all of my life I had never felt so weak. But Bruce is a stoic man. He likes to keep everything moving, and I think he fears that if he stops to look too deeply into some of the loss and unfairness that life dishes out, the reality might derail him. He needed to focus on being our sole provider.

Meanwhile, my mom and I threw ourselves into making my home come alive. We hung family photos and bought flowers for the outside deck, placing them in colorful containers. My mom clipped pink cornflowers and dried hydrangeas from the yard and put them in small vases and cups. Sharing a love of flowers and birds, we found a store called Wild Birds Unlimited where Mom bought a small red cardinal made out of glass with a suction cup to attach to a window. I bought a blue birdfeeder. We also picked up bird food, a book about Midwestern birds, and a pair of binoculars. Some mornings I'd walk into the kitchen and find my mom, binoculars to her eyes looking out the windows with the bird book opened on the counter next to her coffee. That always brought a smile to my face.

We drove around my new neighborhood and found a store that sold beautiful French country furniture. The entire store had warm color tones and a cozy feel to it. I immediately felt at home and started looking around. That day I saw a great French country style kitchen table with a rustic farmhouse feel—made with real barnwood, a distressed cream color to its thick hand carved legs, and a dark brown top. After talking for a while with the owners, I learned that they had an interior decorator. I hired her that day to help decorate my house.

Bruce and I went back during the weekend and bought the table along with a matching bench and four antique green French ladder-back side chairs with woven rattan seats. That set became then, and now remains, a favorite belonging in my home.

My sister Mary showed up to accompany me to my third chemo appointment, along with Mom. It was by far the hardest treatment. I was very glad to have my sister with me because her laughter was the best medicine. It seemed that each time the drug beat me down further than the previous time. The nausea and dehydration lingered for days. Sleep was my dear friend.

Number four—the final chemo session—landed on my sixteenth wedding anniversary. Both Bruce and my mom came with me to that one. While I was sleeping, Bruce left and came back with a bouquet of my favorite flowers. He thought a celebration was in order for the last day of chemo.

For me it was just another day, one I'd much rather forget.

During the ride home, my thoughts turned to the next mountain I needed to climb. Thirty-three days of radiation, and then I could finally get back to living my life.

CHAPTER 10

1972–1974

*M*oney started getting scarce around the house, which meant food was in short supply. Six months after my father left, I turned sixteen. No big fanfare, no sweet sixteen party or special gift. Certainly no sweet sixteen car like the one my friend Debbie had gotten. For me, turning sixteen marked my first chance for independence. I would now be able to get a job. I couldn't wait to have things to call my own, like a job and money. I'd had my eye on the local ice cream and burger joint. I thought it would be fun to work there for the summer, so the day after my sixteenth birthday, I took a job at the Checkered Hut.

My first paycheck was fifty-three dollars, and I was so proud of myself that I bought a pair of striped bell-bottom jeans from Steiger's department store. I also invited Mary and Margaret to the convenience store after I cashed my first paycheck and told them the snacks were on me. They were super excited about that, and I felt proud that I was able to treat them.

Summer came to an end and school began again. I was now a junior in high school. The ice cream shop was closing soon, so I went job hunting and was hired to be a cashier at a local drugstore. I continued to work there two to three nights a week and most weekends until I graduated from high school. The autonomy gave me a relief from home life. Browsing the makeup aisle delighted me now because it was possible that I could buy my own mascara and lip gloss. It made me feel very grown up.

My dad had been out of the house for months now, and his departure seemed more like a disappearance. Nobody seemed to know where he was living. I wasn't sure where the rumor came from, but I heard he was homeless.

Our home began to feel like a rooming house. Everybody came and went as they pleased. There were no curfews, no supervision, no parental figure. My mother was depressed and aloof. When she was physically present, her mind was clearly somewhere else. She'd lost a lot of weight and started taking anti-anxiety medicine. The house became a hollow shell.

Instead of being half full, the refrigerator was now empty most of the time. I didn't make much money, but I'd chip in a little when Mom asked. My father never wanted to see us kids, nor did he help us out financially. In fact, the weekend after my mom asked him to leave, he threw a brick through our front window, nearly skimming my younger sister's head. When I heard the sound of crashing glass, I pulled back the curtain in the picture window and saw him climbing back into the blue station wagon.

Even though I was working and saving money and doing fairly well in school, my self-esteem was plummeting. I thought I was to blame for my dad being gone because I was always pushing my mother to do something about Dad's drinking. Now that she'd taken action, I couldn't help feeling guilty, thinking that maybe I was the one to blame for this family's downfall. My outer shell became hard, tough as nails, but inside self-hatred was eating me alive. I had placed extreme and unrealistic pressure on myself, thinking I could make things right with my family, that if my dad left, everything would be better. I was wrong.

During that time, Sheila and Joan were spending more and more time at their boyfriends' house. They were dating brothers, Jesse and Jamie, and I didn't believe them when they told Mom they were staying overnight at a girlfriend's house—which they claimed on most weekends. Seeing through their lies was easy for me.

Charles was twelve by this point. The lone boy of the family, he spent a lot of his time working on his minibike. When he wasn't throwing fire crackers off the roof of the elementary school with his friends and running from the police, he'd be with older kids at the local hang out drinking beer and smoking marijuana. He came and went as he pleased, just like the rest of us. My eight-year-old twin sisters came into my bedroom often at night to sleep. Mary lived in a fantasy world of made-up stories. Margaret was moody and grumpy. Most of the time, they both looked shell-shocked.

Because we all fended for ourselves, I too did whatever I wanted. It was around this time that I got a boyfriend named Dave. His best friend, Brad, was going out with my best friend, Debra. She wanted to spend time with him, and I didn't want to lose her as a friend, so even though I had a crush on someone else at the time, I reluctantly said yes when Dave asked me out. Weekends were centered on when and where we all could drink beer and Boone's Farm apple wine. Our hangout was located in the woods, and when it got colder, we'd find someone's basement to hang out in. I came home whenever I wanted to, and nobody seemed to notice. There were many nights that I'd wake up in the middle of the night vomiting because of how much alcohol I'd drunk. I skipped days of school and started smoking cigarettes and experimenting with marijuana. And I began to spend more and more time with Dave. He said he really cared about me, and I felt I could lean on him. He was there when I needed someone to care. I began to trust him.

One Saturday morning, midway through my junior year in high school, I approached my mom in the kitchen and said, "I think I'm going crazy." I really thought I was. My body and mind didn't seem to be one anymore. Like an out-of-body experience, I didn't feel present in the here and now and was totally convinced that I was getting whatever Marie had.

"What do you mean by that, Susan?" she asked sounding concerned.

"I mean, things don't seem real to me. I'm living in a fog."

"Do you want to sit and talk?"

"Yeah, sure."

My mom sat next to me on the edge of the same sofa where Marie had sat catatonic only a year before. I sat crossed-legged in a yoga-like position as thoughts ran through my head. *Why was Marie the one who got sick? Could I be next? Am I going crazy now? What if an ambulance comes and takes me away?*

As I lit a cigarette, my mother tried to assert some parental control. "Susan, you're too young to be smoking," she said. I had become rebellious in other parts of life but never smoked at home and was never disrespectful. In this moment, I signaled the end to all of that. I looked at her and said, "I don't care." I really didn't. I didn't care what she thought any more than I cared about anything else. My insides felt dead.

"How long have you been smoking?" she asked.

"It doesn't matter." I took a drag of my cigarette. "Mom, how do we know what Marie has? Maybe all of us could get it."

"You're not going to catch what Marie has," she said firmly. "She has a mental illness that's pretty rare." Not knowing what a mental illness was, I wasn't reassured. I tried to dig for more explanation, and her response was, "Susan you're going to be fine." The message I heard was, *I am not here for you. You're on your own.* I was a motherless child. The conversation ended with me walking away saying, "You just don't understand." What I had wanted was a little compassion; even just a hug would have been enough. It would be many years before I realized that this era marked the start of my panic attacks.

Marie had been evaluated by the health care team at Northampton State Hospital, and there was a meeting scheduled to talk about the plan for her care. In late fall, when my mom had originally asked me to accompany her to this meeting, I'd been reluctant. But I knew she needed support, and because I was the only one able to offer it, I felt I had no choice.

As my mom and I drove up the hilly entrance, my first glance of what I knew was the "mental hospital" gave me shivers. I'd pictured an inviting, white-faced, modern-looking building with perhaps even a pleasant security guard at the front entrance. A place that was cheery and comforting. A place where Marie was happy and getting the help she needed. There was nothing inviting about this three-story, eroding, Gothic-style hospital. Heavy steel bars covered all the windows. *What really goes on in there*? I wondered. This was supposed to be a hospital, not a prison.

Originally known as the Northampton Lunatic Asylum, it housed those with the most severe cases of mental illness and was notorious for its dark past and ghostly stories. There was an unmarked cemetery located on the property where over one hundred and fifty lost souls had been laid to rest. This became my sister Marie's home. She was eighteen years old.

My mom and I followed the lobby signs around to the side of the forbidding building to a small, half-empty parking lot. We parked the car, put our gloves on, buttoned our winter coats, and headed out into the cold. The natural scenery became more visible when I looked down from the hilltop. The trees were so barren they looked like tall matchsticks. The steeple of the Catholic church where my parents had exchanged their wedding vows twenty years earlier peeked up in the distant view.

We walked arm in arm toward the front door. My mom had lost so much weight in the last few months that I hardly felt her small frame leaning on me for support. We walked with our heads down, holding onto our hats so they wouldn't blow off. My mom seemed both mentally and physically fragile to me, and once again I felt the responsibility of the caretaker, the one in the family holding it all together.

We entered the building through a double-wide, heavy steel door and stepped into the front lobby. We were greeted with eerie-like quiet. The words *dismal* and *dark* came to mind. There was no comfort here. I took a deep breath and smelled a thick mixture of pine and body odor that nauseated me. "*What* is that smell?" I whispered to my mom. She didn't answer. A serious-looking woman sat at the check-in desk. Her hair was tied up in a bun, and she wore turquoise reading glasses. I walked up to the desk and said, "Excuse me. We're here to see Marie McNally."

The lady with the blue glasses directed us to a conference room down the long pale beige-colored corridor. This place was creepy. While walking down the hall, I felt like I was about to enter a haunted house, the kind I'd never dare go into as a kid. How could my sister get better in a place like this?

The patients roaming the halls looked nothing like Marie. A guy with long, disheveled red hair, piercing blue eyes, and wearing a bright red blazer stared at me as he walked past us in the hallway. A woman who stood well over six feet tall, with large hands and feet and bumps all over her face, walked swiftly past us, chattering as she went. Her rapid-fire sentences were incomprehensible. My sister wasn't like them. Marie didn't belong here. I desperately hoped that when I saw her, she'd be back to her old self, just getting a lot of rest and biding her time until release. Maybe all of this was just one big bad nightmare.

Mom and I didn't have to wait long before Marie was escorted into the room. A caregiver guided her to a chair holding her right arm, which was restrained in a white, tight-fitting straitjacket. She shuffled in wearing only socks and a pair of blue, hospital-issued, cotton pants that were far too big for her. The sight of my sister in a straitjacket was shocking. "Mom, why does she have to wear that thing?" I asked. I wanted to demand, "Take that stupid thing off of my sister!"

"They must think she's a harm to herself or to others," my mother replied. She pulled some tissue from her purse, wiped her eyes, and then blew her nose.

Marie sat in a chair across from us and next to her caregiver, a heavy-set woman, dressed in blue scrubs from head to toe. Marie sat with her head down, staring at the floor. When she did look up, I noticed that her eyes drooped. She looked heavily medicated, and her long dark hair was a tangled mess. Why couldn't they at least tidy her hair with a ponytail? She continued to open and close her eyes as if on the verge of falling asleep. My mother asked what type of medication they were giving her.

"Haldol, an antipsychotic drug used for acute psychosis and schizophrenia and otherwise known as Vitamin H," the caregiver told us. We exchanged a few words about her treatment and state of mind, and Marie never acknowledged our presence.

The entire medical team caring for Marie included a nurse, a patient care coordinator, and a psychiatrist. All were present today to discuss my sister's plan of care. I figured my mom understood the medical terms because she was a nurse. I was focused on the strait-jacket and whether she was at risk of harming herself or others. Since she'd arrived at this hospital, she'd been very violent toward others, they told us. Apparently, I had been right to be scared that day in my parents' bedroom, curled up like a snail, hiding. They recommended that she stay until there was no further risk of harm but gave no timetable.

My mother asked the doctors if her acid trip could be to blame for her condition, but the doctors couldn't say.

Looking at us through black, thick-rimmed eyeglasses, the psychiatrist said, "Mental illnesses are very hard to diagnose, and we try not to put a label on patients until we have something truly conclusive." Pausing for a moment to consider, he then added, "It's pretty rare for an illness like this that includes catatonic behavior to be caused by an acid trip." He made mention of schizophrenia, and that was the first time I'd heard that word. My mother turned to me from time to time to offer an explanation, but I still didn't understand what any of it meant. She told the doctors there was no history of mental illness or schizophrenia in our family. I was slightly relieved to hear this and at the same time baffled. *Then what the heck is the matter with my sister and how did she get this way?*

My heart broke that day for Marie and for my mom. I saw the anguish and pain in my mother's eyes, and I couldn't do anything about it. *How much pain can one heart hold?* I wondered. I later learned that my mother never really got over that day but relived it over and over again in her mind—the image of her child like that, all bound up—and lived with the guilt of committing her daughter to such a horrible place. After becoming a mother myself, I'd come to better understand the pain she must have felt watching her daughter in this hospital and not being able to do anything about it. At the time, I thought, *This cannot be happening. Please someone, anyone, wake me up from this nightmare.*

Disheartened, Mom and I drove home in silence, a box of Kleenex between us. The tears I cried left my expressionless freckled face salty and seared. We were close to home when my mom thanked me for coming with her. "I know it was hard for you, Susan because it was hard for me, too," she said. "It was hard to see Marie like that." That day, I'd known that I was going to accompany my mother because it felt like the right thing to do. What I didn't know was that this visit would haunt me for years to come. I couldn't erase the memory of my beloved sister with the tangled hair and drooping eyes, wrapped in a jacket of bondage. Marie's life was in the hands of medical professionals, but seeing her in the mental hospital that day destroyed my hope that my sister would ever come back to us. I couldn't free myself from the pain of that, no matter how much apple wine or beer I drank.

*O*n my first visit to the radiation department, located just one floor down from the chemotherapy department, I was handed a hard plastic card, similar in size and shape to a credit card. I called it my radiation credit card, and the nurse informed me that swiping my card at the front desk would mark my presence each day for the thirty-three days.

A few weeks had passed since my final chemo treatment, and it was now mid-November. The issue of trust seemed to be ever-present for me, and here it was again on my first day of radiation treatments. I knew I had to trust the medical professionals who were taking care of me. As a nurse, that was difficult for me. I took care of people, and I was good at it. I was just not good at being taken care of, and I'd find myself apologizing to whoever had to do things for me. I also knew the mistakes that could happen. My breathing always stopped whenever I entered the building of the cancer center, and this day was no different.

I was led to the locker room by the nurse who greeted me at the front desk. She wore light pink scrubs with matching sneakers. I used to like the color pink. Not anymore. Her hair, tightly tucked into a bun at the nape of her neck, gave her a severe look. We stopped at the locker area for instructions—"Take only your shirt and bra off, leave your pants on, put this hospital gown on, the opening goes in the front, put your clothes in any locker, bring your personal belongings with you, and when you're all done dispose of the gown here." She pointed to a large utility basket that said SOILED LINEN on top.

After the locker lesson, the nurse led me down a hallway to the radiation treatment room. A large beige machine that resembled a spaceship hovered over the treatment table. The room was cold and barren. The mold of my upper body that I'd been fitted for a week earlier was made of a hard, dark plastic and sat on top of the sterile table. Music played from a small radio tucked into the corner on a built-in desk. Mellow tunes.

After positioning myself correctly into my mold, the nurse and I exchanged a few words, and then she shuffled out, her rubber clogs squeaking against the tiled floor. The machine started to hum, and a few seconds later the nurse asked me not to move at all. My body remained motionless. I tried to think positive thoughts, but my mind took a trip to the dark side:

Am I supposed to feel this? Because I don't.

Could they have measured wrong?

What if the radiation is hitting my heart and not my breast?

All this radiation can't be good for me. How much am I getting?

How much is too much?

Feeling like a big grizzly bear that had stepped into a trap and was being held captive, my fight-or-flight response kicked in. My heart rate increased, panic mode overtook me, and I wanted to break free. Then I heard the nurse say through the overhead speaker, "How are you doing, Susan?" On other days, she'd say, "Only one more minute left." Her voice, thankfully, had the effect of breaking through my panic.

ON THE SATURDAY morning after Thanksgiving, John and Sarah, who had been visiting for the Thanksgiving holiday, each pulled out a counter stool and sat at the kitchen island. Bruce and I had been reading *The New York Times*, catching up with each other, and drinking coffee. "We have something to tell you guys," Sarah said, with a big grin that called attention to her single dimple. "We're going to have a baby."

John added, "Yup—we're pregnant."

I knew they had been thinking about having a baby, but I hadn't really thought much about it. I'd never wanted to be one of those mothers who bugged their kids about making her a grandmother.

"Oh my God, you're kidding me!" I gushed.

Bruce said, "Wow, that's awesome, you guys. Congratulations."

I added. "That's the best news I've heard in quite some time. I'm so happy for you guys, congratulations!" I walked over to give them both a hug, and Sarah and I both cried. Bruce and John went to the other side of the kitchen to talk. I was surprisingly elated. Because my mind was so preoccupied with all the cancer business, I had to remind myself that other people were living their lives. Sarah was due in the early summer. Now I could really put this cancer stuff behind me and focus on becoming a grandmother. For me to hear that wonderful news when I'd been feeling so low was a true gift of love. Thoughts of a new little baby to hold totally took my mind off the rest of my treatments. I knew I was going to make it.

The January fourth snowstorm brought about three inches of white fluffy snow, and more was predicted. Wearing my white North Face jacket, brown Ugg boots, comfy black yoga pants, a half-zip fleece top from LL Bean, and my favorite wool scarf, I walked swiftly through the parking lot of the David Pratt Cancer Center in St. Louis, headed for my routine eleven o'clock appointment. Already feeling weary, I shivered as the blustery snow blew around me in circles. Finally, the day had come—my last radiation treatment—day number thirty-three.

I went through my routine: swiping, undressing, and catching about five minutes of *The Ellen Show* before my name was called. Today I wasn't in the mood for impersonal pleasantries. The nurse called my name, and while she started walking down the long corridor, flanked by floral prints on the walls, she asked me how I was doing. I don't think she even noticed that I didn't reply. After the final treatment was over, I stopped in the bathroom on my way out and looked in the mirror. My head was bald, my eyelashes were gone, my eyebrows, once dark and full, were thin and sparse, and my face was pale. I was cold and tired, and I felt simply awful. As I walked to my car and felt sleety rain hitting my face, I wished my mom were with me.

The treatments had taken a serious toll on my body. I was always cold, had a pounding headache most days, and I struggled to get out of bed almost every morning, no matter how much sleep I'd had the night before. I now knew what it meant to feel utter fatigue. I desperately missed my mother and wished she were here to take care of me. I'd gotten to the point of relying on her support, but now all I felt was loneliness. My mom had done everything for me while she'd stayed with us, all the things I didn't have the strength to do on my own. She had driven me to all of my appointments. She'd made sure I routinely ate and drank enough fluids. Now even eating felt like a burden to me. Doing this all by myself was unbearably exhausting.

It had been a little over a month since my mother had gone back home. She had been with me for three months, and now I missed her presence. I had reassured her that I'd be fine on my own for the rest of the treatments—but, now I wasn't so sure. I didn't like being alone with my thoughts. I missed sharing my feelings with her and having her tell me it would be over soon and that everything would be okay. I felt proud of myself for finally finishing treatment and couldn't wait to call her when I got home.

This was supposed to be huge day for me—the end of all of my cancer treatments. So instead of going straight home, I treated myself to a stop at my favorite French café. I sat at a table near the window, lifted up my glass mug filled with hot chocolate, and silently toasted myself. *Now*, I thought, *I can get all this cancer shit behind me. It's in the past. I can get my life back.*

Shortly after arriving home from my last treatment, I took a large black Sharpie from a drawer in the kitchen and marked an X on January 4, 2008, on the calendar that hung on the wall in my pantry. Sarah had created the calendar for me out of poster board, saying, "I was thinking you might use this to count down the days." It was a thoughtful gesture, and it had helped me over the months. Sarah had made the first black X in August to mark the start of my chemo treatments. The last X for chemo was on October 19. Then they picked back up again for radiation—thirty-three X's in a row during November, December, and the beginning of January. The concluding treatment on January 4, 2008 was marked with a much larger and darker X than all the rest. I wanted to make a statement with this one. Sarah was right, it had been cathartic to mark off the days.

I'd imagined back in August that this final X would be more than symbolic. I'd seen myself jumping for joy by the time I arrived at this moment. But I was too tired. When I stepped back from the calendar and looked at that big black X, something inside me stirred. It wasn't joy. It was more of a calmness of completion, like the feeling I had when I ran my first 10k ten years earlier. Now I could sit back, be proud of what I'd accomplished and let my body recover. I breathed in deeply, walked to the sofa, and fell sound asleep within minutes with my dog Molly snuggled at my feet.

When I woke up an hour later, I picked up the phone and dialed my mom. I'd promised I would call her after my treatment, and I figured she was waiting to hear from me. She congratulated me for hanging in there and for being so strong.

"I miss you," she said.

"I miss you, too. It's just not the same here without you." I said.

I daydreamed about our time together during my treatments. She pampered me, did my laundry, and even folded my underwear. She made me tea and toast, and there'd always be a fresh glass of Gatorade with ice in it, just the way I liked it, on my bedside table. She'd cover me up with a blanket when I fell asleep watching TV. She listened as I cried with fatigue, reminding me that I'd get better. She knew I loved the feeling of clean white socks on my feet, so she'd rub my feet with lotion, slip on clean socks, and tell me everything was going to be okay. Sometimes I'd wake up and hear her in my room just checking on me. I felt safe knowing that she was watching over me.

My mother's presence also had a positive effect on my family; thanks to her, the household was able to maintain a sense of "business as usual." All of the pieces just fell into place with mom there. She became a mother figure for Samantha when I wasn't able to be there. Samantha loved it when my mom greeted her at the bus stop every day and the time they sat together and chit chatted. Bruce also came to rely on her. When he needed someone to talk to, she was there. And thanks to her presence, Bruce didn't feel so guilty when work kept him away from the house. He had come to rely on her so much that a few days before she was about to leave, he begged her to stay longer.

During those months, my seventy-five-year-old mom's pace was my pace—slow and leisurely, and I cherished our time together. We took walks in the neighborhood and talked about life. She shared things about herself and her upbringing that I'd never known, like the fact that her own parents hadn't been demonstrative with love and affection. No hugs, no "I love yous."

"Why do you suppose your parents never told you they loved you?" I asked.

"I don't know," she said. "I guess it was just all assumed."

She told me about how her parents had slept in separate bedrooms and led separate lives. My grandmother worked full time as a nursing supervisor, and my grandfather was a firefighter who hung out in Irish pubs when he wasn't working. As a teenager, my mother had taken on the responsibilities of meal-preparation and cleaning for the family. Her only brother protected his mother from their abusive, drunken father. They survived as best as they knew how. The similarity of my grandmother's life to my mother's life with my father got me thinking that maybe she thought her husband's behavior was normal. Maybe that was all she knew. Perhaps that was why she waited so long to do something about it. Knowing this made me keenly aware of why, prior to Bruce, I'd always been attracted to guys who didn't treat me well.

One morning midway through my chemo treatments, sitting at the kitchen island having a cup of tea with my mom, I asked her how she had dealt with the craziness that went on during Dad's worst years, in the aftermath of Marie's hospitalization. My mom was a stoic woman and spoke in a passive tone. "I let it roll off me," she said. "I just let it go." She started fiddling with her napkin and added, "I never thought my life would turn out like this. It was what it was, but we had to live with it. It wasn't fun. Your dad didn't share a lot," she said. "He kept a lot inside." She told me that in the early days, before all the kids, that my dad was quiet but happy. They had friends over on the weekends and vice versa. They held and attended neighborhood parties like the yearly Fourth of July celebration, and they became active in St. Mary's Church. On Sundays at church, my dad passed the collection basket for donations at the 11:45 a.m. mass. "Your dad was very generous and well liked," she remembered. "He was only nineteen when his father died."

My mom told me that she thought my dad just kept all of his feelings inside on a simmer, only to reach a boiling point when he was drinking. "Sometimes when he drank, all his sadness would come out," she said. "He'd often stare at the picture of his dad hanging on the wall, repeating 'forty-eight, forty-eight, forty-eight,' while sobbing. I think that haunted your dad for a long time."

I shared with my mom my first memory of her and my dad together: they were walking hand in hand at the New York World's Fair. It was 1964. I was eight years old, walking behind them with my sisters and my grandmother. The flutter of joy I experienced in my stomach that day is one I have never forgotten.

"Yes, we were happy then," she said. "I just don't think we expected to have so many kids. It got much harder after that."

I asked her if my dad had been the love of her life. She responded with an emphatic *no*. Then we finished our tea in silence.

Those months together and those talks led me to feel a new kind of kinship with my mom. Suddenly I understood her and was able to accept that she had done the best she could while I was growing up. I could now see in her much of the love I'd been searching for my entire life. She had finally shown me love, and I reveled in it. I began to feel forgiveness toward her. I no longer blamed her for my awful childhood, and I even began to forgive my father. Neither of my parents had the skills to handle seven kids, and my mother survived the only way she knew how. And so, I figured, did my father.

My mom, an unlikely companion just three months earlier, had finally become my friend, my confidante, and my sidekick. The loving, supportive mother I'd craved for most of my life had come alive before my very eyes. I felt deserving for the first time in my life. "I will always remember our time together, Mom, even if it was because of the breast cancer. You took such good care of me, and that meant so much to me."

"I was glad I was able to do it," she said.

"It brought us much closer, Mom, and for that I will be forever grateful."

"Well, it's over now, Susan, so just try to put it behind you," she said. Her reply jolted me back to another time and place. I was a sad little girl again, sitting on her bed, crying. I needed to hear warm words from her, and I thought that after all we'd just been through together, things would now be different for us. But we are who we are. My mom was more comfortable putting things behind her.

Although the surgery, chemotherapy, and radiation were over, I still had five years of tamoxifen ahead of me. But in my mind, I was done. Now that the heavy-duty part of my treatment plan for cancer was over, I wanted desperately to get back to living my life. I wanted to be in control and not let this cancer define me. This was the beginning of the time that I recognized my world would never be the same. My life suddenly became divided into two parts—before and after cancer.

I didn't have to go right back to work for the money, but mentally I needed it. I liked going to work every day. Work held a sense of purpose for me, and I felt that I made a difference in patient care. I liked being the boss and holding other nurses accountable for the care of their patients. I wanted my old life back.

So, in between chemo sessions, which was when I usually felt my best, I searched the local hospital websites, looking for nursing manager openings. In between my second and third chemo treatments, I'd scheduled an interview for a nursing manager position of a postpartum unit at St. Anthony's Medical Center, a large community hospital about a half hour drive from my house.

The day of the interview was a brisk November day, and temps dipped into the forties. As I was getting out of my car, the wind almost took the door off, along with my wig. *Whoa!* I thought, *that would be embarrassing.* I was self-conscious of "the look" people would give me if they saw me with no hair. It was the pitying stare, the half-smile that said they felt sorry for me. Avoiding those looks was the reason I'd bought the two wigs in the first place, plus it was winter, and my head was cold. But today wearing the wig was important because on this day, I simply wanted to be a nurse looking for a job.

Back in August, when I'd first become bald, I'd walked into the elevator at the hospital and a little girl about three years old couldn't take her eyes off me. The little brunette girl with chocolate brown eyes and the cutest purple-and-pink outfit kept saying, "Mommy, why doesn't that lady have any hair?" I smiled at her, but she looked scared of me. I was sure that my baldness combined with the pallor of my face were unfamiliar and disturbing to her. Her mother whispered, "I'm so sorry," but I wasn't offended. I love children for their honesty.

I worried about discrimination should I disclose my cancer to the new job prospect, so I said nothing about it. I walked to the front entrance of the hospital and, before entering the roundabout door, I checked my image in the glass reflection. Indeed, my wig was off a bit. The bangs were crooked. I quickly straightened up and walked toward the elevator with my little secret.

When I entered the office of the vice president of nursing, I told her assistant that I was there for an interview, and then took a seat at a small round table with room for four. I placed my cranberry-colored leather business tote on my lap. Inside was my favorite soft brown leather planner. I loved this bag. Whenever I used it, I felt extremely professional. Its design included several pockets to hold things like pens, cards, an eight-by-eleven-inch yellow legal pad, and a datebook. It zipped all around and kept everything under wraps, nice and secure. As I rubbed the engraved initials "SFM" on the outside, it brought a smile to my face. I loved the fact that two Christmases ago, when Bruce bought this business folder for me, he'd made it extra special by having my initials engraved on it. It was the first time I owned anything personalized, just for me.

Marge came out, greeted me, and then gestured toward her office. "Nice to meet you Susan, please take a seat," she said. I sat in one of the two flowered chairs directly in front of her desk. The rest of the room was nearly bare. A dark brown mahogany book case with a matching credenza sat off to the side. A watercolor print, matching the hues of the carpeting and chairs, hung to the right of me on pale blue walls.

Marge wore a black business suit with a white ruffled blouse. Her three-inch black pumps pushed her to six feet tall. Her shoulder-length, light-brown hair was neatly pulled back behind her ears, and she wore full makeup. I handed her my resume, and she pulled out her zebra print reading glasses to look it over. After a few minutes of silence, she looked up at me and said, "Pretty impressive resume."

"Thank you," I replied. We started with the basics—what brought me to St. Louis, where was I from, why I wanted to work there.

Instead of telling her that I really wanted to work at the large teaching hospital where my husband worked, I said, "I'm looking to move up in my career, and I know that there's a management position in women's health open here."

"Yes," she confirmed, "there are actually two positions." I was applying for the postpartum manager, which wouldn't have been a move up for me, but it was all I'd seen available on the hospital's website. I was immediately intrigued by this new information.

The other position was director of women's services, which would require me to oversee the entire staff in the women's services department: labor and delivery, postpartum, and the special care nursery units. Now *that* would be a move up. We skipped over the original interview and skipped right to discussing the director position. The entire interview process would take another week and included a personality test, interviews with staff members, other managers, the director of labor and delivery, and finally the CEO of the hospital.

After two weeks, Marge asked to take me to lunch. We drove to a nearby Italian restaurant that was all decked out in green, white, and red. We placed our food order, and while we waited, she offered me the director position. I was elated. I would start just three days after I finished my radiation treatments. The breast cancer wasn't in charge anymore. I was!

About a month into my new job, I was riding the elevator alone when a young woman who looked to be in her early thirties got onto the elevator. As we rode up, she turned and said, "I like your haircut." I thanked her, recalling the little girl I'd met on an elevator one month ago who'd been afraid of me because I had no hair. Now I was hiding my baldness under my wig. At that moment, I realized that it didn't matter what others thought of me or my hair. Hair or no hair, I was no longer willing to hide my true self. So that weekend, I ditched the wig and went to a local hair salon where I had my gray speckled hair, which now covered my entire scalp with about an inch of hair, colored a dark caramel brown. I felt like myself again. I decided never to wear the wig again.

Monday morning arrived, and I picked out the pair of diamond stud earrings that Bruce had bought me for Christmas. I'd be making my debut at work with very little hair, but at least my ears would sparkle from the diamond studs, I thought. I suspected that walking into my first day with this dramatic new look would elicit a lot of stares, and I was right. They lasted for about a week, after which most people just smiled when I'd walk by. When I ran into Marge, she said, "I would have hired you anyway."

I shared my health story with my closest work friends. Then it quickly became my norm. The freedom of coming out was exhilarating. I walked into my first meeting and took a seat at the long conference table that held twenty-plus people. I looked up from my brown leather planner and noticed a woman about my age smiling at me from across the table. She said, "I look like that, underneath this." And then she pointed to her own head.

Her name was Patricia, but she had asked me to call me by her nickname, "Beez." We stayed after the meeting and became instant friends. She shared with me her own breast cancer journey, which was on par with the timing of mine. She, too, was a director of a department, so we attended a good number of the same meetings, and we became inseparable at work. Whenever I was in the vicinity of her department, I'd stop in and we'd catch up. Sometimes I'd moan a bit about the cancer and its ongoing side effects. She'd also share with me her aches and pains.

Three months into the job, springtime arrived in St. Louis. As I walked through the parking lot one beautiful crisp day, I took in deep, grateful breaths of fresh spring air. I loved the smell of the new mulch where beautiful flower beds had just been planted. Pink, yellow, and purple pansies in large clay pots lined the front entryway. I stopped at Beez's first-floor office. "I am freaking exhausted," I huffed, plopping into an office chair. Seated behind her desk, she said, "Me, too." Her office was a safe haven for me where I didn't have to put up a front of strength. We were able to shoot straight when we were together, and we gave each other strength and confidence.

A few months after meeting Beez, I ran into her at a meeting. She was no longer wearing the wig; instead, she had a pixie cut like mine. I loved it and was proud of her courage. She told me. "I decided to be brave like you."

*I*t was now the summer of 1973, right after finishing my junior year of high school, and just when I thought life might get better around the house now that both Marie's craziness and my father's disruptive drinking escapades were no longer part of daily life; but things only got worse. The whole family was feeling the after effects of the alcoholism and mental illness tornado, and nobody was around to help pick up the debris left behind by the storm. We were all shell-shocked, left to fend for ourselves and trying to survive the best way we knew how as kids.

Mom had just lost her job at the women's clinic where she had worked for the past five years. What I didn't know until many years later was that she had become addicted to Xanax, the medication her doctor prescribed for her stress. She'd been fired because it must have affected her job performance. At the time, I noticed that she was still losing weight, and her eyes drooped, which gave her thinning face a constant worn-out look. She took a nursing job at another hospital, working full-time at night, and when she wasn't working, she slept. That meant that I hardly ever saw her.

I was excited to finally be a senior in the fall because after that I'd be able to move out of the house. I had even started thinking about where I'd like to move to; I was just thrilled at the idea of getting out. I'd turn eighteen in July, just one month after graduation. Every day one thought persisted: *I'll be able to do anything I want. My mother can't stop me. My father doesn't care. I'll finally be free.*

Sheila's pregnancy announcement came when she was five months along. She was seventeen. September was having warm spell. The air was wonderfully warm and dry, and the wind blew my hair like a low-speed fan. Senior year had just started. I was walking fast to the bus stop to catch a ride home from school, hoping to speed past the verbal garbage the creepy construction workers always hurled at me when I walked by. From behind a chain link fence, grown men in hard hats gawked, whistled, blew kisses, and made suggestive comments about my clothes. They weren't scary, but they were upsetting. *These men probably have daughters of their own*, I thought with disgust. *If only I had my own car like my friends, I wouldn't have to worry about this crap.*

When I made my way to the intersection of Main and State Streets, I glanced up at the second-floor office window of my dad's former law office. Often in the past, I'd seen him sitting there, with only the back of his head visible. Just knowing he was sitting there at work used to make me smile. I loved that Dad. He wasn't drunk. He was the head of a functional family. Today, when I looked up, the office was empty. I wondered where he was and what he was doing. *How must it feel for him to no longer have any contact with his entire family?* I wondered.

When the bus arrived, I climbed the steps, put my quarter in the meter, and took a seat near the front like I did every school day. For the entire forty-five-minute ride home, the only thing I thought about was my twin sister and the situation she'd gotten herself into. Sheila hadn't been to school in over a week and wouldn't tell me why. It was now three weeks into our senior year, and I wanted answers.

Her behavior had changed over the recent summer months, and we hardly saw each other anymore. She was always hanging out with her boyfriend, Jesse, who looked like a blond Rick Springfield. His straight brown hair hit the top of his shoulders, and he was a true rebel. My hair-ties were always missing, and I knew he'd taken them to hold back his ponytail. His very presence annoyed me. He was an unemployed high school dropout who had nothing better to do than hang around our house. I told Sheila I thought he was a loser and that she deserved better. "I don't care what you think," she told me.

We used to share everything, Sheila and I. The same room, the same clothes, our thoughts, our feelings. Now she hardly spoke to me, and she always walked around with a frown. Her big brown eyes drooped like those of a sad puppy dog. She wouldn't dress in front of me anymore, and one day I realized that her sudden modesty could mean only one thing: she'd gotten pregnant. We were connected in the special twin way, and I knew she felt trapped and depressed. She just sat on a chair in the dark basement most days, staring at the TV and smoking cigarettes.

I arrived home after the long bus ride and went looking for my mom. She was unclipping shirts and towels from the rope clothesline in our backyard. The sky was a beautiful bright blue and filled with white puffy clouds. For days I'd been desperate for my mother to confirm Sheila's pregnancy, and day after day, she sidestepped the subject. But today, my mother turned to look at me as she placed the neatly folded clothes into a wicker basket. "Sheila told me today that she and Jesse are going to get married."

"Are you freaking kidding me?" I asked, trying not to scream. "You're not going to let her get married, are you?"

"She told me that's what she wants," my mother said. "And, you were right, Susan, she also told me that she thinks she's about five months pregnant." Pissed off by my mother's passivity, I yelled, "She is *seventeen* years old! She has no idea what she wants or what's good for her. *You're* the mother," I said. "Tell her she can't get married. You're supposed to help her when she's in trouble!" My face was burning hot, my heart racing as I yelled, "She *cannot* have a baby! She's going to ruin her life. What is the matter with you?!"

There was a lot of shame surrounding teenage pregnancy at that time, and I grasped for ways to convince my mother. "How is she going to graduate from high school?" She didn't answer me. I continued. "How is she going to raise a kid? She doesn't have a job, Jesse doesn't have a job, and he's a loser, Mom."

My mother's response was always the same. "She told me that's what she wants." Then she added, "She and Jesse are just going to have to figure it out together."

Sheila and I had planned to move out of the house together after we graduated. We'd talked about getting an apartment together and going to college somewhere, anywhere, to get the hell away. Now what? She was screwing everything up. We'd had this planned for so long. Now I hated her.

I was fuming. *They'll figure it out?? Yeah, right. Jesse is a loser. She can't marry him. I'm going to make her change her mind. Unfucking believable. My mother is unbelievable. How could she let her seventeen-year-old daughter get married? Does she just not give a shit?* I'd never felt so angry, but somehow I was feeling furious, helpless *and* still hopeful that I could stop this runaway train. After that confrontation, I lost all respect for my mother. I despised her passivity.

When I found Sheila, she was sitting downstairs watching TV as always. She told me the same thing my mother told me, that she was going to marry her boyfriend of only six months. And, yes, they were happy and were going to have the baby. She said it all so nonchalantly that I knew she wasn't telling the truth. She sure didn't look happy. When I asked her if she was sure that's what she wanted, she said yes, but I could tell from the way she stared at the TV, refusing to look at me, that the truth was, she felt trapped with nowhere to turn. Sheila had already given up on herself.

Jesse was also seventeen and very immature and self-absorbed. He never wanted to discuss any plans with Sheila. Therefore, she made all the arrangements for their approaching future together. She picked the date and time of the wedding, found an apartment to live in, and even found Jesse a job at McDonalds. She started buying clothes for the baby. When he *did* come around, he was always fussing with his dirty brown hair, shaking it back and forth or combing it. He never made eye contact with me other than to ask me if I had a hair tie. I told Sheila that I thought she was crazy to get married and that she was way too young for any of this. Before I stomped out of the room, I barked that I would not be attending the wedding. She didn't say a word.

Slamming the door behind me, I sat on the floor of my bedroom in front of my record player. Looking out my dormer window, all I wanted was to fly out of it like a bird and be free. I wanted relief from the nightmare I was living in. Thank God for music. It offered escape with the flick of a radio dial or the drop of a needle on vinyl. Getting lost in Diana Ross and the Supremes, Cat Stevens, and The Beatles gave me brief reprieves from all the craziness of my upside-down life. I'd listen to songs like "Wild World" and "Ticket to Ride" and lose myself in the lyrics that were clearly written just for me.

A month later Sheila married Jesse, and I reluctantly attended to support her as maid of honor. Then she moved out of our family home and into a low-income housing project. Four months later, she gave birth to a healthy baby girl. It was January 1974; the same year Sheila and I should have been celebrating our graduation from high school.

Joan's pregnancy announcement came a few months after Sheila's. Joan was more or less the middle child, number four out of the seven. She was fifteen years old. She was afraid to tell my mom that she too was pregnant, afraid it would push our mother over the edge. Later, when I asked Joan about that time, she would tell me that she'd had thoughts of ending her own life because she didn't know what else to do. She walked around the streets instead of going to school during the day, contemplating just how to finish herself off.

Finally, when Joan could no longer keep it a secret, Mom approached her and asked, "Joan, is there something you need to tell me?" She was six months pregnant by then, and the father was the brother of Sheila's new husband.

Because she was so young, Joan spent the rest of her pregnancy about a half hour from our house at a home for unwed mothers, run by nuns. Joan didn't have a choice; my mother made the decision. I think my grandmother also had something to do with it because she knew some of the nuns there. The plan was that Joan would give up her baby for adoption, but eventually she decided that she couldn't follow through with it. Jamie, the sixteen-year-old father of the baby, didn't have much say in the situation. Giving up her baby for adoption, I thought, was the reason she'd been sent to a home for unwed mothers. But when she came home a few weeks before her due date, she informed my mother she'd decided to keep the baby. I shouldn't have been surprised that my mother let her make that decision, yet I was. "If Joan comes home with that baby, I'm moving out," I announced.

So just two months after my first niece was born, we welcomed a second baby girl into our family. It was the beginning of March, 1974. To this day, I don't know why my mom asked Joan about her pregnancy but didn't confront Sheila. Was it their age difference? Joan was only a year and nine months younger. Joan ended up living with my mom after her baby was born; Mom became a kind of surrogate mother to Joan's baby girl, Amy. To this day, Amy feels that my mother played a big part in raising her. Sheila, on the other hand, struggled to get by, going on Medicaid and eventually raising her daughter, Heather, by herself.

During this time in my life, I had no understanding of what the hell was happening to my family or why. I'd thought that after my father left, things would get better. I thought we'd all come together and support each other after the chaos. I was wrong. The damage was already done. Everyone kept to themselves and hid their wounds well. I was also deeply embarrassed by my family. First it was my father's alcoholism, then my older sister's admittance to a mental hospital, and then my two younger sisters' pregnancies and babies. I never discussed any of it with anyone, except for my boyfriend Dave. When my friends asked why my sisters hadn't been around, I lied and said they were sick. But the rumors got around, and eventually I had to tell the truth. We were *that* family.

In school, everyone seemed to be staring at me; it was as if I was the one who was pregnant. Shame became my unwanted friend while denial became my needed friend. I withdrew further into myself and spent a lot of time fantasizing about how I wished things could be.

The embarrassment I had of my family would eventually become ammunition for Dave to attack my sense of self-worth. He had gotten good at telling me what I should do and how he was going to save me from my "screwed up family." And I listened to him.

I started living in an imaginary world during my home economics class. We learned how to balance a budget, to cook, and to sew. My favorite part of the class was life skills. We were taught how to manage life outside of high school. We learned what the price of an apartment and a week's worth of groceries may cost and what types of bills we'd be responsible for. Our final assignment was to build a book of the life we envisioned after high school, with a budget to go with it. This book became my lifeline to the outside world, the one I wanted so desperately to be a part of.

I was sure that college would save me. It would take me away from the craziness. I'd be able to reinvent myself in an all-new environment. I'd start a new life that wasn't filled with chaos. Just me alone, making my way in the world. I envisioned myself walking on a beautiful college campus with tall brick buildings, green grass all around, and large maple trees. The kind of trees that give so much shade you can sit and stay cool on the grass underneath and just daydream. I imagined kids my age all around, laughing and enjoying life. I saw myself walking to class, books in hand, smiling.

That dream was soon crushed. My guidance counselor informed me that, because I hadn't taken any college prep courses, I wouldn't be able to attend a four-year college. My only choice was a community college.

Despite that the future didn't look particularly bright, I was happy when it was time to graduate. When I arrived home on the night of my graduation, there was no fanfare; only a small, round graduation cake that read "Congratulations" sat on the kitchen table. There were no cards, no presents, and someone had already eaten a piece of the cake. Still, being finished with high school was symbolic of the next phase in my life, and I would find a way to move forward one way or another.

CHAPTER 13

2008–2011

E mma Susan arrived kicking and screaming on an exceptionally warm summer day, June 25, 2008. Weighing six pounds, eight ounces, her tiny nineteen-and-a-half-inch body was simply perfect. She had long black hair, dark eyes, and curly eyelashes that fluttered when she looked at me. Just like twenty-eight years earlier when I first held my newborn Sarah, when I cradled baby Emma in my arms, I thought my heart was going to explode.

A week before Sarah's due date, my suitcase sat packed and tucked in the corner of my closet. On a Tuesday night, Sarah's husband John called to tell me that Sarah's water had broken and that they were in the hospital. Even though no labor had started, I knew that she'd most likely deliver in the next twenty-four hours. I booked a flight for the following morning.

The next morning as I prepared to leave for the airport, I got the news that Sarah's pain was so intense she called for an epidural. And after twenty-four hours of labor without much progress, the decision was made to have a cesarean section. So it turned out that while I was flying over Ohio, a new little new person entered my life, changing it forever.

For me, becoming a mother had been wonderful, but it came with a lot of stress. It meant being responsible for teaching my children to fly on their own and to become independent, conscientious, young adults who knew right from wrong, made sound decisions and built self-respect, and could support themselves. But now, as a grandmother, I didn't feel any of that stress, which made the experience that much more rewarding.

The flight from St. Louis to Bradley Field, near Hartford, Connecticut, lasted a little over three hours. I took the time to reflect as I looked out at the puffy clouds. Sarah and I had talked about her delivery ahead of time. She was a private person and wanted it to be just her and John in the delivery room. Bruce and I would be on standby if they needed us, and I think it comforted our daughter that Bruce was an obstetrician who had trained with and knew Sarah's doctor well. During my nursing career, I'd been involved in deliveries where there were many family members present, but I'd always thought that going through a birthing experience was important for just the couple.

When the plane landed, I called John who told me brief details about the birth and then handed the phone to Sarah. She was groggy, and her voice was deep like it always was when she was tired or sick. I told her to get some rest and that I'd be there soon. The drive from the airport to Springfield, Massachusetts, was a little over a half hour. I hopped into my rental car and started on my way to The Family Life Center at Mercy Hospital. The car ride on this beautiful summer day through the winding back roads of rural Connecticut took me past farms with white fences and horses grazing, fruit stands open and selling strawberries, and the smell of fresh mown grass. I loved the East Coast and was glad to be back where it actually felt like home. I couldn't stop smiling, wondering what this new precious bundle of love looked like.

This hospital was one I'd worked in for five years, so I knew my way around pretty well. I'd made a lot of friends during my time there. My buddies Kathy and Kelly were at the front desk when I walked through the automatic door. Although it had been over five years, seeing them was both awesome and awful; it was wonderful to see them, and it made me sad to realize that they were no longer part of my life. I genuinely missed their friendship and camaraderie and all the laughs we used to share, and I felt regret over not keeping in touch. Life had gone on for all of us. When they congratulated me on being a grandmother, I suddenly felt old.

At fifty-two I was more than middle aged. I had never imagined what my life would be like at this age. For as long as I could remember, I'd been focused on raising children. I kind of lost track of myself. Where did all those years go?

As I walked down the sunny hallway toward the future of my ancestry, past phases of my life began to play in my mind like a movie montage. I suddenly became aware of my own mortality. I thought of my breast cancer and what I'd be missing if I weren't here to see this miraculous moment. Suddenly everything became radiant. The yellow daffodils, purple irises, and pink peonies in the garden outside the window came into crystal clear focus. I wanted more of these moments. As if by a windshield wiper, my past felt like it had been just flicked away—creating a new clean slate. I wanted the rest of my life to matter. I wanted to make more memories. I instantly felt the urgency to live.

I tiptoed into Sarah's room and was immediately overcome with emotion. Sarah was lying with her eyes closed, and John was asleep in a chair that turned into a bed next to her. Both were covered in white cotton blankets. Although the sun was still shining outside, the room was dark, with curtains closed, and quiet, with Emma sound asleep in a clear bassinet at the foot of the bed. At first, I felt like an intruder, and then Sarah opened her eyes and said, "Hi, Mom."

My daughter had just given birth—to her own daughter. As I made my way to the bed to hug my daughter, I glanced at Emma and I could almost physically feel my heart expanding. This was a love I'd never felt before, yet it seemed so familiar. Something was welling up inside of me, an intense enthusiasm for life. I fell in love all over again. I'd heard that becoming a grandmother was wonderful in countless ways. But to experience it in my own way now simply took my breath away.

I loved this baby already, deep down in my soul, just as when I had given birth to Sarah. She was an extension of Sarah, of me, of both of us. She had my blood running through her veins. The fact that Sarah gave her the middle name "Susan" was precious to me. Nobody had ever honored me in that way before.

Although I wanted to pick up Emma right away, I needed to make sure Sarah was okay first. I walked to Sarah's bedside, stood next to her bed, reached out to caress her forehead, and said, "How are you, sweetie?"

"I'm good, just tired," she said.

"I am so proud of you, and Emma is absolutely beautiful." I hugged her and then John. They were now a threesome.

While they both took turns telling me the details about the labor and delivery, I picked Emma up from her bassinet and immediately started crying. Caressing her perfect tiny hands and toes reminded me of the moment I first held Sarah. A new life, a new birth. I wanted to stay here forever, to revel in this wonderful feeling. I was absolutely content, and nothing outside this room mattered. I felt a rejuvenating spark. All I thought about was being a grandmother to Emma and how I wanted to marvel in life's little moments all over again. I'd just become the family matriarch, and I was determined to be a good one.

After Sarah had Emma, I wanted her to celebrate the milestone of becoming a mother. I wanted to be there for the questions she had, teach her what I had learned the hard way. I wanted to give her the compassionate support and love that a mother needs from her own mother. Tenderness, love, guidance, advice—all things I was denied. I wasn't going to be the kind of mother who let her daughter down.

Before I knew it, it was time for me to go home to St. Louis, leaving Sarah's new family behind. I called Marge and tried to get some more time off, but that would have meant giving up my summer vacation the following month on Martha's Vineyard, and Sarah knew that the Vineyard was my favorite place in the world. "I'm going to be mad at you, Mom, if you don't take your vacation. You and Bruce always look so forward to it." Somehow, as Sarah spoke—standing at the kitchen sink in her pink fleece bathrobe, her shoulder-length brown hair clipped in a messy bun on top of her head, rinsing out baby bottles—I didn't believe her. But I needed to abide by her wishes. John was taking more time off from work, and the two of them would handle it, she said. Sarah was always stoic in that kind of way. She hid her emotions well.

I left Sarah's home feeling apprehensive, but knowing that Sarah and John were together in this new world called "parenthood" brought me solace. As long as they relied on each other, they would be fine. As I pulled out of the driveway and waved from my rental car, I saw Sarah turn away, rubbing her eyes. I knew she'd miss me, and that broke my heart. The sadness I felt as I drove to the airport came out in a river of tears. All I could think about was how soon I'd be able to return.

THE RINGING OF the phone cut through the sound of Steely Dan playing on the car radio as we drove over the Golden Gate Bridge. Bruce and I were on our anniversary vacation in late October, driving to Napa Valley on a beautiful crisp fall day. He answered the phone, and it was Sarah, who wanted to tell us that she was pregnant for the second time. Emma was almost four months old. Although Sarah and John had talked about having more children, this was a surprise for them. Bruce handed me the phone, and Sarah's voice sounded both happy and concerned. Her maternity leave for Emma was coming to an end, and she was returning to her full-time teaching job. She wondered how she was going to handle two babies a little under a year apart. I said, "Don't worry, I can help you."

Eight months later, on June 22, 2009, just three days before Emma's first birthday, Ethan Michael was born. He was undeniably perfect. He weighed a little more than Emma, but he looked much bigger. His sparse hair was light brown, his skin paler, and he had an extraordinary pair of hazel eyes. Two grandchildren! I hadn't known that this type of love existed beyond my own children. Oh, the pride, the joy, the calmness of being a grandmother. My love was doubled now with the birth of a second grandchild.

I stayed for a week to help out and desperately wanted to stay longer. But I had only one week off, so I focused on when I could return, even if it were just for a weekend.

Three months later in September, we visited again. Ethan cried when I picked him up. He seemed afraid of me, didn't know me. I cried too and my heart broke. I wondered, was this what it was going to be like from now on? Visiting every three months, perhaps every six months? *How are they going to get to know me?* It bothered me that I'd miss all the in-between stuff, the little things. I missed my grandbabies terribly, and I wished I lived closer to them.

Something unforeseen had shifted in me, and I felt unsettled. Just like a year earlier, after Emma's birth, I started rethinking my priorities, questioning what I was doing and why. Why was I working full time? Why did I go back to work so quickly? A part of me had wanted to jump right back into my old life—a job I loved, challenging but rewarding with friends at work and a feeling of contentment in my life. That's what my old life did look like, but I was different now.

It had been six months since Ethan was born, and I'd started to get a little antsy on the job. Work as a director was challenging, and while I enjoyed it in the beginning, I was finding it harder and harder to focus on my work. All I could think about was how Sarah was doing with Emma and Ethan and how big they were getting. I wondered what new things they were learning, what they were eating, whether they were sleeping through the night.

Then, I got a new boss named Shelly, and we clicked right away. She was in agreement with what I was trying to accomplish on my units and became my biggest supporter. She had a sensitive side to her that I enjoyed seeing. Suddenly, I was reenergized. Because I had spent the early part of my career working part time to raise children, I decided to give myself at least two more years in the job and then reevaluate. It would take me at least that long to make the changes I'd envisioned at work.

My monthly meetings with Shelly kept me going for a while. I made more work friends, felt successful, and was proud of myself. I actually enjoyed going to work every day.

The present model of care at St. Anthony's was old-fashioned—the same level of care I'd experienced when I'd had children thirty years earlier. I'd never been satisfied with this, especially since it didn't support the family unit, breastfeeding, bonding, or education for new parents. My major initiative was to turn the departments that I was in charge of into family-friendly units, the kind I'd been trained in some seventeen years earlier.

The staff had been pretty reluctant for change, so I faced a lot of resistance. I enjoyed the challenge for a while, but then I realized I just didn't have the desire to fight the battles anymore. The job was just not fulfilling me the way my other job had. The pride and passion I had felt for my job at Yale New Haven Hospital was just not there. This job wasn't the same, the people weren't the same, my life wasn't the same, and my energy level wasn't the same. I no longer had the stamina to see the entire project through to completion. And my family was growing again.

I was walking toward my gate to board a plane to Connecticut when my phone rang. My son Patrick was now twenty-nine years old and living in Hartford with his fiancée, Emily. I answered the phone and heard the sound of my son sobbing on the other end. He and Emily had just welcomed their own little human being into the world. Ava Elizabeth was born on May 26, 2011. My third grand-child. Life had never been better. Goosebumps went through my entire body and seemed to fly right out of the top of me. Through sniffles, I congratulated them both and said that I'd see them soon. Patrick had told me about six months prior that he and Emily were going to have a baby. I was over the moon. Patrick had never been happier, and Emily seemed like a perfect match for him. Now I felt content knowing that my two adult children had each found some-one wonderful to share their lives with. But I began to feel even less sure about that promise I'd made to myself to stay on the job another two years. Two years suddenly seemed like a very long way off.

Not long afterward, Bruce and I sat at a conference table with our fairly new financial adviser, Bob. We had met him only once be-fore and liked him. Our meeting began as the first one had, warming up by talking about our personal lives. Before talking about financial stuff, we discussed our private lives. I liked the personal touch. He started with Bruce. "So, how's the new job going?"

"Great," Bruce answered with a big grin. It had been about two and a half years since he started, and he'd just made partner. One of his professional goals had always been to be a partner in a private group of doctors, and now he was. He had also received a consider-able raise, which was fantastic because Bruce always worried about money.

Bob turned to me and said, "Sue, how's it going with you, and your job?"

I surprised even myself when what came out of my mouth was, "I hate my job." I continued on, saying that my job was just not what I thought it would be, and now after becoming a grandmother, my career didn't matter much to me anymore. "I just feel like I'm wasting my time, when all I want to do is to be with my new grandbabies and spend more time with my youngest, Samantha, while I can."

Bruce looked at me with wide open eyes and said, "Wow, Sue, I didn't realize you felt like that." For the next hour, we spoke about me, my life goals, short term and long term, my health, my feelings about stress and the job, and how I wanted zero stress in my job. I told them that I had thought I could go back to my old life and that my work life would feel as it had before. But now that I'd come to the realization that it wasn't going to happen, Bruce and I agreed it was time for a professional change. Breast cancer had changed me. It had changed my priorities.

We then talked finances and long-term retirement planning. I had never planned on not working. I never wanted to be financially dependent on anyone. But my life with Bruce was more than secure, so the writing appeared on the wall: Bruce's raise equaled my salary, so if I stopped working, there would be no loss of income. Within a month of that meeting, I turned in my resignation. I left my job in June of 2011 and never looked back.

I was suddenly excited about what my life could be. Although we still lived in St. Louis, having the freedom to travel when I wanted and to also be home for Samantha after school meant everything to me. She was now seventeen and would be a senior in high school soon. There was one thing that had stood out while I was going through my cancer treatments: I wanted to prioritize spending time with the people I love.

CHAPTER 14

1974–1979

*T*he summer after my graduation from high school, I sat on the edge of my bed, ruminating over my recent predicament and pondering the direction of my life. I couldn't go away to college, so my dream of getting the hell out of Dodge was that, only a dream. *What am I going to do now? I'm stuck.* Carole King's "It's Too Late" played on my record player. Dave, my boyfriend of almost three years, had asked me to marry him and I'd said yes. But I didn't love him. And he was violent. When he got angry, he lashed out with his fists. The first black eye came with excuses just like the others. He was so sorry, begging for forgiveness and swearing that he'd never do it again. I tried to believe him each time a dozen red roses arrived at my door, but my gut was telling me not to marry this guy. I was already tired of being on the receiving end of his volatile temper, but there I was agreeing to spend the rest of my life with him. *Why would anyone in her right mind agree to more of this? But what if I go crazy like Marie? Would he take care of me? And what if I didn't get married to him? Where would I go? What would happen to me?*

Dave was the only person in my life giving me any attention, and he promised he'd take care of me. He offered me protection from what he called my crazy family. He promised a home, security. He had a steady job and promised to support me. How could I say no to that? Wasn't it better than nothing? My college plans had fallen apart, and I no longer had Sheila to make plans with. I thought, after all, I was the one with all the problems, not him. I was damaged goods. Maybe I was getting a good deal.

Although the decision went against my better judgment, I felt stuck, so I decided to marry Dave. I bargained with my thoughts; he promised to try to control his temper, and I promised myself to do whatever it took to get out of my house. What I would learn years later was that I would remember that moment of resignation every time I had to make an important decision. I promised myself that I would never again go against my better judgment. But it would take a long time to get there.

The wedding took place six months after my graduation from high school. After Dave and I got married, we lived in the second-floor apartment of a two-family house about ten blocks from my family home. I attended the local community college for one year, hoping that I could become a dental hygienist, but that would have required another two years of school. And my SAT scores had been low, so I didn't get into the program. Instead, I settled for the one-year dental assistant program.

The fall after my graduation from Springfield Technical Community College, I took a job as a dental assistant in a private dentist's office. I hung in there for six months and then quit. I hated the job and wasn't fond of the bossy dentist. Over the next few months, searching for jobs became fruitless. I floundered for a bit and eventually became totally financially dependent on Dave. This was an all-time low for me. The sad truth was I didn't even want to get out of bed in the morning.

Contact with my mother at this point was sparse, and I still had no contact with my father. I kept in touch with Sheila and saw Joan only when I visited my mother on the occasional Sunday. My brother Charles liked to hang out with Dave, so he was at our place a lot. So were Mary and Margaret. Marie stayed at the state hospital for close to a year and spent her twenties in and out of psych hospitals, and I lost contact with her. She eventually transitioned to a halfway house and then her own subsidized apartment. A social worker helped keep her on track and followed up with her every six months—and to this day still does. As long as she takes her meds she remains well.

Dave's father knew someone who worked at the grocery store—Stop and Shop—and the guy offered me a job as a cashier. Thrilled, I jumped at the opportunity. When I'd been a little girl, there was one Christmas when the only thing I had wanted was a cash register. Now I was going to play cash register for real. I would start the following week, in the spring of 1977. Dave graduated from high school two years before me, and rather than attend college, he had worked a minimum wage job in the same factory that his father did, making cardboard boxes. When we married, he started working for the city, driving trucks and plowing the city streets in the winter months. It wouldn't be until many years later that I'd understand the significance of my accepting that grocery store job.

When I was twenty-one, Dave and I bought my grandmother's one-bedroom, Cape style home on a quiet residential street. She offered us a good price, so we couldn't resist. It was a cute place—a golden yellow color with white shutters and a fenced-in yard.

We moved in, and I made it a home. Owning a home felt spectacular. For the previous two years we'd had to put up with a brutish landlady and no access to a backyard. With the new home came a beautiful backyard with plantings and flower beds. I frequently sat outside on a lounge chair listening to the birds sing while enjoying the privacy. No more people peeping at me and watching my every move. I bought green plants for inside and made a garden of fresh lettuce and tomatoes outside.

Dave and I had all the floors sanded, put a fresh coat of paint on the walls, and wallpapered the kitchen a small yellow-and-gold checkered pattern. I bought yellow curtains to match. A hope chest sat at the end of my bed, which I'd dressed in a brown-and-blue comforter with matching pillow shams. The flowered dishes and yellow glasses I'd picked out in a magazine and glued into the dream life book I'd created during my senior year of high school sat in my kitchen cupboard.

Dave fixed up the basement, and we put our stereo and television down there. We even bought a used pool table. We'd have friends over on Friday and Saturday nights, watching the Blues Brothers on *Saturday Night Live* and staying up late playing pool. Life felt good. But not for long.

The insults and the unpredictability of Dave's moods came in spurts. When I sensed his irritability coming on, I tried to stay out of his way. Once the mumbling started, I knew it wouldn't be long before insults and belittling would be hurled my way, and then a slap to the side of my head, always reminding me it was my fault. The inevitable apology followed. "Please forgive me, Sue, I can't live without you, please don't ever leave me. I don't know what I'd do without you." A dozen red roses would unfailingly arrive the following day. This went on for three years.

The trust that I had in Dave eroded to some degree with each disagreement we'd have. He'd throw my own words back at me—personal thoughts about my fears and insecurities—and use them to his advantage. And before I knew it, I started believing the things he said. Looking back on it now, I realize it was a form of brainwashing: you hear over and over again that you're worthless, and you start to believe it because you have nothing to grasp on that tells you otherwise. First it was the name calling, then demeaning comments about my family, and of course, about me. Nothing was ever his fault. My vulnerability became his strength, and my self-esteem plummeted with every slap, kick and punch. One evening after a big fight with Dave, I left the house, walked around the neighborhood, and ended up in the backyard of my family home. In the dark, I sat on the swing just as I had as a child, sobbing. I had no one else to turn to. I swallowed hard, stepped into the back porch and opened the back door. I walked through the kitchen and found my mother resting on the sofa in the living room. The volume on the TV was on low, as were the lights.

I sat at my mother's feet, at the end of the sofa. She looked like she was sleeping, but I wasn't sure because the television was on. I whispered, "Mom, are you awake?"

She opened her eyes slowly. "Susan, what are you doing here?"

"Can I come back home? I just had a really bad fight with Dave. And . . . I don't want to live with him anymore."

"What do you mean, you don't want to live with him anymore?"

"I don't think I should have married him, Ma. I don't love him."

"You need to give your marriage a try," she told me, without asking for any details.

"Why? I don't want to be married to him anymore," I replied. Distraught and disheartened, I told her that we were having a lot of fights and that for the past three years I'd tried, but now I wanted out.

"Some marriages take work," she said. I wondered what she would have said if I'd told her Dave was hitting me, that he was the one who gave me black eyes during my senior year of high school. *But,* I reasoned, *how could she not know? Please see through my lies, Mom, I am in pain here and I need loving and comforting. I don't want to go back there.*

This was the one time I had asked my mom for help, and she offered nothing. Then I went upstairs and saw that Joan had taken over my bedroom. I went into the backyard for a while and sat on the swing again. This time the sobs came in gasps—I couldn't catch my breath. I was a motherless child pretending to live an adult's life. No childhood home to turn to, no marriage. I felt broken and as lost as I'd ever been.

As I walked across the lawn in the dark, I saw Joan and her toddler through the kitchen window. There was no room in the inn for me.

Walking back to my house with blurred vision from the tears, I hoped a car or lightning would strike me dead. At least that would end my lifetime of pain.

When I got home, Dave asked where I'd gone. When I told him I'd gone to see my mother, he let me know right then and there, "It's me or your family. You can't keep running back to them; your mother doesn't care about you, Sue." Believing his words made me feel like a wounded bird. I couldn't fly back home. Feeling I had no choice, I accepted my marriage. There was nowhere else to turn. From that day forward, guilt and shame directed my decisions. Denial navigated my way.

Within a year, I was pregnant, and I threw all my energy into motherhood. With my belly growing, my unborn baby became my lifeline to love. I couldn't wait to become a mother. I was twenty-two years old.

Early Sunday morning, October 28, 1974, my life began to change. The contractions started in the middle of the night, and by early morning they were in high gear. I got out of bed. A dream of mine was about to come true, and I was terrified. I couldn't wait to become a mother. Even though I was already three weeks past the due date, I couldn't believe it was actually starting to happen. Then I wondered, *Is this what labor feels like? How much worse is it going to get?*

After I took a shower, Dave started tracking the contractions which were now coming every four to five minutes. The last one before I left the house for the hospital turned my belly rock hard and took my breath away. I held onto my bedpost for support until it subsided. I called my doctor and he told me to head into the hospital. During the twenty-minute ride to Baystate Medical Center, I rubbed my stomach in a circular motion with each contraction and wondered if my mother had done the same thing when she was in labor with me.

Trying to breathe as the Lamaze teacher had taught me didn't ease the pain. I'd never felt anguish like this before. I was trying to be brave and breathe through the contractions, but I was becoming more and more scared. If this was just the beginning of labor, I was terrified of what the rest of it would feel like. I'd heard such horrible stories about the suffering during labor that, frankly, I didn't know what to believe. I started questioning myself—would I be able to do this?

I urged Dave to pull up to the entry, come in with me, and move the car later, but he refused. He wasn't one to draw attention to himself, so he dropped me off and went to park the car.

"I'll meet you in there," he said.

On my way to the front doors, I stopped twice and clutched a nearby railing to steady myself during the contractions. As I bent over the railing, with my breathing on the verge of panic, I felt like a child again, scared and alone. I thought of my mother and desperately craved comfort from her. I prayed for somebody, anybody, to take this pain away. On the brink of hyperventilating, I continued walking as my whole body shook with fear. Holding onto Dave would have been so much better than holding this cold railing. All I really wanted was for someone to tell me that everything would be okay, but there was no one in my life who could do that for me.

I made my way inside, holding onto my belly. At the registration window, I answered all their questions and the admission was complete. As soon as Dave arrived, we headed to the labor and delivery unit.

The contractions intensified as we rode the elevator to the birthing area. As I gripped the arms of the wheelchair, I struggled with the increasing pain. I was hooked up to a baby monitor in the labor room and was immediately comforted to hear the baby's heartbeat. It sounded beautifully strong. Then, all of a sudden, the heartbeat slowed to a beep . . . beep . . . beep. What was happening? Then just as quickly as the baby's heart rate slowed, it returned to what sounded like normal to me. A friendly nurse who stood at my bedside had said, "It's okay, maybe the baby was just lying on the umbilical cord." She then told me she was going to examine my cervix to see how far I was dilated. Three centimeters. *Are you kidding me? There are seven more to go?*

A few minutes later, in the middle of a contraction, I heard the baby's heart rate go down again, and in an instant, a flurry of activity in my room. In addition to the two nurses, there were three more strange faces in the room, all staring at the fetal monitoring tracing. Concern was written all over their faces. Because I didn't understand what was happening, I started crying. Then I looked over at Dave who was sitting in a chair at the right side of my bed. He looked like I felt.

Another contraction and the heart rate went down again. I did a couple of position changes that the nurse had asked me to do. Then, she put a green oxygen mask on my face, and I didn't understand why. Was I dying? This time, my baby's heart beat didn't go up, in fact it got slower and slower.

The nurse removed the IV bag from the hanging pole and placed it on my bed. "Susan, we're heading to the OR. We're going to have to do an emergency cesarean section because your baby is under stress and needs to come out now." I looked at Dave through the green mask, my eyes calling out for help. He had a shocked expression on his face and was completely silent as he was asked to stay behind.

In the operating room, I was given an epidural to numb my lower half and was then placed on my back. Everyone was scurrying around but silently, which spooked me. Urgency was in the air. I'd come to find out many years later, as a labor and delivery nurse myself, what they were actually doing and why the urgency. It was called a crash section; they were rushing around to get the baby out as quick as possible because her heart rate kept dropping. At that point, every second counts.

In my wildest dreams, I'd never imagined that something bad could happen during childbirth. "Are you doing okay?" the anesthesiologist asked from behind my head. With a screen blocking my view of the operating site, I lay on a cold operating room table with my arms stretched out to the sides and strapped to arm boards. A green oxygen mask strapped around my head blew cool air into my lungs. There was a bag to catch my urine and wires all over on my chest. I was half-naked, alone, numb, crying, and close to vomiting. I thought to myself, *Is he fucking kidding me right now? Am I doing okay?* As I'd been taught to do all my life, I lied about what I was feeling and simply nodded yes.

Someone suddenly removed my hospital gown. I was now completely naked in front of all these people. I felt everyone in the room staring at my pregnant naked body, and I was mortified. Why was everyone so damn quiet? There was an undeniable urgency in the air. *Now I am really scared. Am I dying? Is my baby dying? What is happening?*

A nurse came to my side wearing a surgical hat and mask. It was hard to understand her speech through her mask. She asked me if I knew what was happening, and I replied while gasping through tears, "No."

She explained the situation in one short sentence: "The baby's heart rate is very low and he or she needs to come out . . . now."

"Can my husband come and be with me?" I asked. Despite Dave's shortcomings, we relied on each other and over the past five years had become mutually dependent. But the nurse told me this was an emergency, and they didn't have time to go get him. I prayed for my baby and for me. I repeated the "Hail Mary" over and over again. Then I switched to, "Our father, who art in heaven . . ."

Suddenly, I felt a tugging in my belly. I started to have a hard time breathing and began vomiting. Then I heard the doctor say, "Oh shit. It's like pea soup." *What does he mean by that*? I heard a noise like suctioning and then, "It's a girl!" Then complete silence.

The baby wasn't crying, and I started to panic. *Why is it so quiet in here?* The same nurse came over and told me that my baby was having a little trouble breathing, and they were bringing her to a special nursery to get evaluated. And then there she was, my seven-pound, three-ounce baby girl. She was swiftly wheeled out in an incubator with an IV attached to her bruised scalp. They were bringing her to the Neonatal Intensive Care Unit. "Is she going to be all right?" I asked.

The nurse gave me a textbook answer: "They're going to take good care of her." As usual, I was left uncomforted in a time of great need.

I was not prepared for a caesarean section, never mind the issues with meconium staining and its effects on a baby's lungs, which I was soon to learn about. Meconium is stored in the baby's intestines until after birth. I was past my due date, so the baby had matured enough that her intestines had started working, which resulted in a bowel movement inside of me that turned the amniotic fluid a greenish-black color. Breathing in the meconium blocks the respiratory passages, making it hard for the baby to breathe. Some babies develop pneumonia. All of this was completely foreign to me. Strange as it may sound, although I now realize how unprepared I was for motherhood, at the time, I felt as prepared as I should have been.

Awake now in the recovery room with the epidural worn off, I felt I'd been sliced across the middle. I'd never in my life experienced this much physical pain. I never thought birth would be a traumatic experience. Everything I ever saw in magazines and on TV showed perfect pink babies handed to smiling mothers.

The neonatologist came to my bedside and told me that Sarah had swallowed some amniotic fluid that had thick meconium in it, and added, "You'll be very lucky if your daughter survives the night."

My thoughts ran wild. I couldn't cope with the possibility of losing the baby, the only bright spot in my life. I hated him for being so cocky and nonchalant. What kind of doctor terrifies a patient, especially a young, inexperienced, new mother? I had never once considered that I might not leave the hospital without a healthy baby. And now I actually thought my baby was going to die. All I could think to do was pray; "Please God, help my baby make it through the night."

Sarah's X-ray came back clear the next morning, revealing that she did not have pneumonia. The doctor said that they had gotten her out just in time—before she could breathe more meconium filled fluid in. Her prognosis was good. They told me the best thing for her was to breastfeed.

"Sarah Catherine" was the name I had already picked out for a girl. "Catherine" after my grandmother. The morning after her birth, when I held my child in my arms for the first time, I felt a happiness that I'd never before imagined possible. I told her through tears that I loved her and that everything was going to be all right. I now knew what it was like to believe I would die for someone else, because I instantly knew that I'd give up my life for Sarah. I wondered if my mother had ever felt that way about me.

Halfway through my first week home with Sarah, my nipples became sore and cracked. I really had no clue about breastfeeding. I wondered if Sarah was getting enough milk, and already I was starting to feel incapable as a mother. Dave was no help; he just kept telling me to call the doctor. Instead I called my mom. She had worked as a nurse on the maternity unit for a number of years, but her response was simply, "I'm sorry, Susan, I didn't breastfeed any of you. I can't help you." I could feel her reply hit like a dull thud in my chest. Just like when I'd asked her if I could come home and she had refused me.

Being Sarah's mother became the most important thing to me. I did not want to be an unengaged mother, so I educated myself about parenting. I relied on Dr. Spock's *Baby & Child Care* book, and the books *The Womanly Art of Breastfeeding* and *The Nursing Mother's Companion.* I hadn't known anyone who had breastfed, so there was nowhere to turn for advice. So my Mary Higgins Clark novels which had been my usual nighttime reading were now pushed aside in favor of these new lifelines.

Over the next year, I mothered Sarah and I mothered myself, reveling in all the beautiful little moments that are brand new to a baby. We read stories and went for long walks. I never felt more alive. I loved being a mother. My world revolved around my child.

My mom moved to Cape Cod around the time Sarah turned one. It was three hours away by car, and because I didn't own a car I saw very little of my mother for the next five years.

When my three-month maternity leave was up, I decided to go back to work part-time in the evenings. Dave would be home with Sarah at night. Although I'd enjoyed working for Stop and Shop, I'd always wanted a career in the medical field, nursing, specifically, so when Sarah was about eight months old, I made an appointment to meet with an adviser at Springfield Technical Community College. Together we came up with a plan of which courses I'd need as prerequisites before I could apply for nursing school. I was initially overwhelmed by the lengthy list, so the counselor encouraged me to take one course at a time, and that's what I did for the next two years.

My life involved taking care of Sarah, working part-time, and going to school part-time. Life with Dave had become a little more bearable. Sarah coming into our lives seemed to mellow him a bit. The violence subsided for a while, like we were living in a honeymoon phase. Life felt good for a while, and after about a year or so, we started talking about having another baby.

$\mathcal{T}$he arrival of June brought with it the same anxiety every year. It was the month of my initial diagnosis, and it was also the month during which I had one of my bi-annual visits with my oncologist.

Dr. Nettles entered the room, breezed over to the counter and picked up my patient chart. "Any issues?" he asked abruptly.

"Well, I'm having trouble with my memory, my brain still seems foggy, and my mind just doesn't seem to want to function. You know that part of your intellect that's responsible for simple math calculations—whatever that is—mine isn't working." I was doing my budget the other day at work, and my brain just could not do a simple multiplication.

"How old are you again?" he asked.

"Fifty-three," I answered.

"It's probably just your age. That happens as we get older." *Bullshit!* I thought. I smirked inside and thought, *Did he just blame my age? What an ass.*

"I don't think that's it," I replied. "That can't be the reason; it happened so quickly." He blew off my responses, and I was so taken aback by his lack of interest that I said nothing.

He told me to lie down on the examination table and then opened my gown, exposing both of my breasts. He listened to my lungs with his stethoscope, palpated my neck, checking for swollen lymph nodes, and then palpated my left breast. Suddenly, his cell phone rang from the pocket of his white lab coat. "I'm sorry I have to get this," he said. I was so done with him and his cockiness at this point that I'd actually thought of getting dressed and walking out. Minutes went by before he returned to the exam room and said, "Okay, everything looks great. We'll see you next time." I wish I could say that I was shocked he never even bothered to check my right breast, which happened to be the one that had the cancer. But I wasn't. And I just wanted to get the hell out of there; I never brought the error to his or anyone else's attention.

Because my treatments had ended, I'd thought it was the perfect time to find a new oncologist. I was finished putting up with Dr. Nettles and his condescending attitude and horrible bedside manner. Dr. Benson came highly recommended from a nurse who worked with Bruce. Her office was closer to home, and I liked that she was a woman.

There was absolutely nothing special about my new oncologist's office. Chairs upholstered with a forgettable pattern lined the perimeter of the waiting area. A coordinating printed set of love seats sat in the middle of the room. Side tables with out-of-date magazines were strewn about. People sat in silence, lost in their thoughts. A television ran the local news. The examination room was equally typical. The exam table, covered in white paper that came from a large spool located at one end and with a flat pillow on top, stood in one corner. A rolling blood pressure machine lingered nearby. A couple of side chairs were tucked together in the other corner. I sat in one, placed my tote bag and sweater on the other, and checked my phone messages as I waited for my doctor.

Dr. Benson opened the door and greeted me with, "Good morning," as she walked over to the computer and turned it on. She was about five foot six, had short, dark, wavy hair, wore very little makeup, and was neatly dressed in Eileen Fisher-type clothing. She struck me right away as a no-nonsense, down-to-earth woman, and I quickly became fond of her. She asked the routine questions: Are you still on the tamoxifen? Any side effects? The answers were the same. Yes. And yes. I was on the tamoxifen and had been for a little over two years. The side effect that bothered me the most wasn't my stiff joints. It was the feeling of living in a sea of fog that never lifted. I'd expected that after I finished the chemo, my thoughts would get more precise and that I would be able to articulate the correct words when I needed them. That never happened. Now I knew why a friend of mine who'd had breast cancer five years ago decided to take her chances of recurrence and discontinue tamoxifen: too many side effects. Dr. Benson and I talked about switching to another drug. It may have other side effects, but it might help with my fogginess. I agreed. We'd reevaluate after a few months.

During that appointment, we discovered that we had a lot in common, and we clicked right away. We were close in age, and both loved Martha's Vineyard and had family living in Massachusetts. And her bedside manner was completely unlike that of Dr. Nettles. She actually listened to me, and her caring undertone was something that I really needed. Her next question took me aback. "Are you depressed?"

After a long pause, I nodded my head and replied, "I think so." I'd been feeling down and had recently started having nightmares, but I didn't think that my sadness was noticeable to others. I was already taking antidepressants and had been since Samantha was born, and I thought that should have been plenty to prevent me from getting depressed. But I later realized that depression doesn't work like that.

Dr. Benson told me about a medical study from Canada which showed that 77 percent of breast cancer patients experience depression within two years of diagnosis. She also explained that, in addition to the trauma of receiving a breast cancer diagnosis and the depressing questions of mortality that it raises, many of the treatments patients receive can trigger depressive symptoms. Hormonal fluctuations are a common cause of depression, and the hormonal changes caused by anti-estrogen therapies like tamoxifen can push a patient into depression. I wondered, *what happens to somebody like me who already has the depression gene? Do I go on more medication? Will my depression get worse than this?*

"I have someone I think you should see," she said, handing me a card with the name of a therapist written on it. Tears welled in my eyes. I felt exposed but also cared for— someone was actually looking out for me. What a relief.

The following day I set up an appointment with the therapist for the end of the week. Her name was Carol, and our entire first session focused on my family and my upbringing. Part of me wished we could have fast forwarded through that part, as it always conjured old deep-seated wounds. Try as I might to will those wounds to be healed, they wouldn't cooperate. And, like unhealed wounds, mine started oozing blood again.

For about two months, I saw Carol weekly. As my hands fiddled with a paperclip I had picked up on the side table, I talked about the loss and pain of my childhood. Again. It was like looking out a train window, watching the stages of my life rumble by. I traveled through all of the grieving stages again—denial, anger, bargaining, depression, and acceptance—and not all in that order. The psychological stress of digging it all up again took me back to a time and place I was way too familiar with. The stress and trauma that my body had experienced were still inside of me, as if frozen in time.

I was a despondent child, a lost teenager, a lonely young adult. Nightmares were frequent, along with free-floating anxiety. And a feeling of panic often sat in the pit of my stomach. Now during my therapy sessions, the gate that held back the pain of those memories was starting to open.

Thoughts raced through my head: *Is this normal? Why do I feel so scared? Why was I having nightmares of my childhood? Why was I feeling like a little girl curled up in the fetal position wanting her mommy?* I was fifty-three years old, and here I was teetering on the edge again, week after week crumbling into tears and then trying to climb up from the exhaustion that followed. Would I ever finish mourning the loss of my childhood?

For two months, I felt exhausted, bluer-than-blue, and emotionally fragile all at the same time. And even though Samantha and Bruce were around, I felt lonely. I'd started rocking myself to sleep at night. It was as if my body had kept track of this rocking motion as a comfort all these years—and now, here it was kicking in automatically, knowing that I needed comfort. I felt the urge to hold onto something, just as I had as a child when I used to hold Little Miss No Name.

I remembered the chocolate brown teddy bear I'd bought over twenty years earlier when I'd first started therapy after leaving Dave. I'd gone to the Vermont Teddy Bear Company, and when I entered the store, I felt joyous. It was as if birds were singing to me. I loved teddy bears. I'd never had one as a child, so I decided that it was time for me to buy one. There were so many to choose from—honey or maple colored, vanilla or chocolate colored, special occasion or themed bears. I conjured the ten-year-old in me and thought about what she would have liked. Browsing through rows and rows of teddy bears in all shades of brown, I saw up on the highest shelf a chocolate brown bear with her head turned looking directly toward me. She was the one, with moveable arms, legs, and head. I picked her up and hugged her to my chest. A halo of safety surrounded me. She reminded me of Little Miss No Name. Now, twenty years later, I found the bear, who'd been sitting in my study untouched for years and started sleeping with her at night. I wanted to take her into my therapy appointments with Carol, but I was too embarrassed, so she waited for me in the car.

After two months of seeing Carol, my nightmares lessened, and I was now taking daily walks. My emotional frailty disappeared from sight. I felt strong enough to stop therapy and focus on living my life.

By this time, Samantha had her driver's license. We'd bought her a car for her sixteenth birthday so she could make the half-hour drive to and from school on her own. For the next few months, I reveled in the luxury of sleeping in until eight thirty and enjoying the peace and quiet of my house in the morning. I'd pour a second cup of coffee and watch a morning show. I started journaling again. Reflection came easy, but I still had a lot of questions about my physical and mental responses to stress. *Will I ever get over the trauma I experienced in my childhood? How will the stress related to my childhood and the trauma of my young adult life affect my long-term health?*

Then my sleep became troubled. For someone who usually fell asleep as soon as my head hit the pillow, insomnia now became the trigger for me to reconnect with Cindy, my previous therapist from Massachusetts. The heaviness that had recently taken over my body suddenly made it difficult for me to get out of bed in the morning and move forward. Although there was Carol, Cindy knew me the best, and I just didn't have the energy to explain my family history and everything else to a stranger again. Cindy knew all the details. We discussed EMDR (eye movement desensitization reprocessing) and I kept an open mind. She said she'd do a little research and see if there was anyone in my area certified to do it.

I met Jean two weeks later and after speaking with her learned that EMDR therapy helps your brain process thoughts and feelings as it did before a traumatic event. You don't forget what happened, but you don't relive it over and over. You still have feelings about it, but they're not as intense. Although I wasn't keen on having to relive traumatic memories, I tried to remind myself of the importance of a saying I'd once heard: "You have to walk through the pain to get to the other side." I'd been experiencing symptoms related to PTSD for

a while, and I wanted them gone. I had especially noticed my insta-
bility a week earlier when Bruce tapped me on the shoulder, and I'd
just about jumped out of my skin. The exaggerated startle response
wasn't the only issue. I'd been irritable and anxious. Both of these
feelings, I knew from the past, were symptoms of my depression returning. At night I lived a life of horrible nightmares.

Jean had become my beacon in the dark. By my fourth month of
therapy and a handful of EMDR treatments, my emotional fragility
and weeping ceased. I felt stronger and less depressed, and I found myself laughing again. I took longer walks through the neighborhood. I
even dug out my 35 mm camera and started taking pictures again. I felt
ready to get back to life without therapy, and during my last session, I
promised Jean that I would return if I felt I needed a lifeline.

Now feeling better, I still wanted to know more about why the
stress of my breast cancer set off such a wave of sorrow inside me.
What was the trigger that brought back the past that I'd thought was
long tucked away? I never wanted to be that depressed again. I remembered how I'd filed away the information I'd found when I was
first looking for causes of my cancer. Now my curiosity led me to
back to that research. I found an article that suggested a cancer diagnosis may trigger cognitive and emotional responses that relate to
patients' prior trauma experiences. After reading that, I sat back in
my chair, crossed my arms and got lost in the thought. *Is that what
happened to me? Do you mean my body has held onto all these emotions and my cancer diagnosis brought it all back?* I understand
now why I'd still been rocking myself to sleep.

My mission of self-discovery continued with more and more
reading. One beautiful golden day in early October, I took my laptop
to a Starbucks and sat outside, deeply breathing in the cool, autumn
air. I reread the articles about adverse childhood experiences and
stress, and then searched online for additional articles. I discovered
something called the ACE study.

Although I had come across some other studies on adverse experiences in childhood, this was a new find, and it changed my way of thinking about almost everything. I devoured the lengthy research paper, which addressed how childhood misfortune can lead to cancer in adulthood. Extremely stressful experiences in childhood can alter brain development and have lifelong effects on health and behavior.

The article was from a 1998 issue of the *American Journal of Preventative Medicine* and was called "Relationship of Childhood Abuse and Household Dysfunction to Many of the Leading Causes of Death in Adults: The Adverse Childhood Experiences (ACE) Study," by Vincent Felitti, Dr. Robert Anda, and colleagues.

Drs. Fellitti and Anda's goal was to determine people's level of exposure in ten categories before the age of eighteen. Each question answered *yes* counted as one point. The highest score was a ten. These are the ten categories:

1. Emotional abuse (recurrent)
2. Physical abuse (recurrent)
3. Sexual abuse
4. Physical neglect
5. Emotional neglect
6. Substance abuse in the household (e.g., living with an alcoholic or a person with a substance abuse problem)
7. Mental illness in the household (e.g., living with someone who suffered from depression or mental illness or who had attempted suicide)
8. Mother treated violently
9. Divorce or parental separation
10. Criminal behavior in household (e.g., a household member going to prison)

This study revealed a powerful correlation between emotional experiences as children and adult emotional and physical health. The higher a person's ACE score, the greater risk to their health throughout their life. For instance, a person who answered yes in four or more categories was *twice* as likely to develop heart disease and cancer and three and a half times as likely to develop chronic lung disease as a person who'd answered no in all categories. I'd answered yes to seven of the ten categories.

I'd always thought that the cause of my anxiety, panic attacks, and depression was related to my upbringing, but I had nothing to prove it. *Was it possible that my awful childhood had caused my cancer?*

I read that incidents in a dysfunctional household don't occur in isolation; for instance, a child does not simply grow up with an alcoholic parent or with domestic violence in an otherwise well-functioning household. But I already knew that. What I didn't know was whether my sensitivity had made it all worse.

The study explored the makeup and functioning of the human brain. I found the information that explained how stressors affect certain parts of the brain during development remarkable. A poorly regulated stress-response system seemed to be at the core of the problem. This system has a profound impact on immune and inflammatory responses because all of the components of the immune system are influenced by stress hormones.

I compared it all to seeing a wild animal in the woods. If I'm taking a lovely nature walk and then suddenly come face to face with a wolf, my body will react because my brain sends a signal telling it to. My heart pounds, breathing increases, pupils dilate, and my psyche knows that I'm either going to fight the animal or run from it. This is known as the *fight or flight* response. The body releases stress hormones, adrenaline, and cortisol. That's a normal reaction.

When the stress goes away, the body returns to normal. But what happens if that wolf lives with you, and you experience this type of fear every single day for years on end?

For many years, people have debated whether nature or nurture more strongly influences the people we become. As more and more studies are conducted, we can definitely say that there is no separating the two. We're shaped by both.

CHAPTER 16

1981–1984

*T*hree months shy of Sarah's second birthday, I became pregnant for the second time. Unfortunately, the mellowness that Dave had exhibited after Sarah's birth had begun to wear off, and our arguments escalated during the latter part of my second pregnancy. It didn't seem to matter to him that I was pregnant—he still came after me with vigor. He wasn't happy that dinner was not sitting on the table when he got home from work at 4:30. I'd make sure that by 4:00 I'd start tidying up Sarah's toys which were usually scattered about the living room. I saw a happy setting for our child; he saw a mess. The kitchen always needed last-minute tidying, so I'd quickly wash the dishes, wipe the counters, and make sure the table was clean. But it didn't matter what I cleaned or left unclean; he always found something to complain about, and he always blamed me for it. He also didn't like that I put Sarah above everything and everyone. He didn't like that at all.

One evening in early fall, I was making his lunch for the following day, just as his mother had done for him. He said, "Make sure you put crackers with peanut butter in there. You didn't do it yesterday." Then without warning I felt a jabbing pain in the back of my right leg. He'd thrown the plastic wrap box at me full force, adding, "And wrap 'em up tight." I looked down and saw that my leg was bleeding. The jagged blade edge of the box had cut me. I was stunned. He used to yell at me when I was pregnant but hadn't laid a hand on me in five months.

"You're such a jerk," I yelled at him. "Finish making your own lunch." And with that I went to my bedroom and shut the door behind me. He didn't follow me.

Fall came and went. It was now the beginning of February—two months before my due date. It was Groundhog Day, and Punxsutawney Phil had predicted six more weeks of winter, which I wasn't happy about; the cold was already lasting way too long. By then, Dave had worked in construction for about two years, and when the weather turned cold, he had less work, which meant more time at home.

There was a cesarean birth class being offered in the evening at my doctor's office, and I wanted to go. This would be my second cesarean, but I still felt I'd benefit from going. I'd spoken to my doctor about having a vaginal delivery, but he was old school—once a cesarean, always a cesarean. He wasn't even willing to talk to me about the information I had researched about vaginal birth after cesarean, and because I was too far along to change doctors, I agreed. I also thought if Dave came with me and everything went as planned, he'd be able to be in the operating room with me during the birth. I didn't want to be alone and scared this time.

Dave wasn't crazy about the idea, but he respected the doctor's advice that I should take the class and decided to go with me.

The class started the second week of February on a Monday night. Sarah was spending the evening at Dave's parents' house. She was their first grandchild, and they were always excited to have her. Whenever I packed up the diaper bag with her pajamas and stuffed Snoopy dog, I'd find myself wishing that I had parents present in my life. As we drove to the class, he noticed a young woman walking along the road. Because he had to swerve slightly around her, he blurted derogatory comments. "What a bitch. Why is she walking in the street when there is a sidewalk right there?"

I yelled at him, "Why are you so freaking mean? What if that was me in the road? You never, ever, have anything good to say about anyone." The fight swelled until I demanded to get out of the car. Then I realized it was February and too cold for me to walk. We spent another ten minutes arguing with the car idling at the curbside until we realized that we were about to miss our class. Later we drove home in silence, and the incident helped to open my eyes to what kind of person Dave really was. What I saw, I didn't like. His behavior confirmed what I already knew: Dave was a miserable, mean person, and he wasn't going to change. I felt like a racehorse who had been wearing blinders, blinders that now seemed to disappear overnight. I now saw his disapproving glares and heard his condescending tone and rudeness and the way he reduced me with his words and hands. That's when I started to think about leaving him.

Although he groaned about it every Monday night, we made it to the remaining three classes, and Dave was by my side on April 5, 1982, when Patrick came into the world kicking with vigor and weighing in at a healthy seven pounds, eleven ounces.

The week before our son was born, Dave and I had been discussing baby names. Because we didn't yet know the sex, we had the name Dave Jr. picked out if the baby was a boy, Lauren if it was a girl. But the more we talked about it, Dave said, "I really don't want the baby to have the same name as me. I have the same name as my father, and I don't like being called 'Little Dave.'" I was relieved because I didn't want him to be forever reminded of Dave. Clearly I was already beginning to imagine a life without him in it.

The day after Patrick's birth, there was a record-breaking blizzard that dumped seventeen inches of snow in twenty-four hours. I didn't mind. I'd had few hospital visitors, leaving me with lots of time alone with my boy. And there was something wonderfully calming about looking out the hospital window and seeing the wind bellowing and the snow falling. I was able to rest and learn how to breastfeed once again without interruptions.

We'd outgrown our house even before Patrick was born, and we knew we needed to move. Dave liked a two-family home close to his parents' house. He figured we could rent out the other half, so the property would serve as a good investment. I said I didn't care, but I actually did. I just couldn't speak up for myself. I'd wanted a small Cape Cod like the one we already had, but with an additional bedroom. I liked the privacy that a single-family home provided. Dave, of course, didn't care what I thought.

It wasn't until I came home from the hospital that I discovered that Dave had already moved forward with the sale of our home. I was financially dependent on him and felt I had no choice when he asked me to sign off on the purchase and sale. He handled all of our finances. Even though I had a job, I handed over my paycheck to him every week. The only things I could buy without his knowing were groceries. Every once in a while, I'd buy a potted plant or mascara or some new hair ties—anything to feel a modicum of independence. But then Saturday morning would roll around, and Dave would sit at the kitchen table, quizzing me about every expense.

Because it would be six months between the sale of our first house and when we could move into the two-family house, Dave found us a dark and dingy first floor apartment owned by a friend. The cranberry-colored exterior paint was peeling, the mustard-colored doors were ugly, and we had no driveway. The place was musty and broken down. And it was dark. Even on a bright day, the sun entered only through the back-kitchen window and only at dusk, and I could feel the darkness all the way to my core. I spent my days taking care of the kids, taking them out for walks, breastfeeding Patrick, and resting when I could. But on most days, I felt sad. I didn't realize until many years later that I had been suffering from postpartum depression.

Unlike after Sarah's birth, Patrick's birth didn't lead to better days between Dave and me. I hated Dave for forcing me to sell my grandmother's house. He'd tricked me and had taken advantage of the fact that I was preoccupied with giving birth and taking care of Sarah. If I had known about his plans earlier, I would have stopped the sale. But none of that mattered now. His continuing belittling, the under-his-breath comments, and controlling ways were enough to provoke a saint. Soon I tired of his behavior and told him so.

One Saturday morning while I was in the bedroom, Dave came in and started getting dressed. He was full of himself, and his dark mood matched his selfish personality. I told him it wasn't right for him to make the decision for me, to move and sell the house my grandmother had generously let us buy at a much lower price than it was worth. He blurted out harsh unkind words about me and my family. He told me he did it for us, which was untrue. I never wanted to buy a two-family house and be a landlord. He knew that. He did it because it's what he wanted. I blurted, "That is just not true—you're full of yourself—you think you know everything." He looked at me with narrowed eyes, shook his head, and while pulling up his pants over his legs said, "You're so ungrateful." Walking out of the room, I said; "Really? Maybe what *you* think is wrong, and *everyone* else is right. Did you ever think of that? You *always* think you're right, you're so cocky."

Whatever positive feelings I'd developed for Dave over the years were now gone. I had no love left for this man. He was always unhappy about something, and it became harder and harder for me to be around him. In fact, I'd never felt this type of hatred in all my life. I loathed his presence, and before long something changed in me. When he'd start an argument, I'd fight back. I told him I hated him. Being a mother had given me confidence and courage. I became a tiger protecting herself and her young.

After six long months in the crappy apartment, we moved into the two-family house. We occupied the second floor, and a single woman and her young son rented the first floor.

Three months later, in January 1984, Patrick had an ear infection and I was exhausted. Dave came in through the back door scowling, which meant that trouble was on the way. I took note of our surroundings. A medicine syringe sat in the kitchen sink along with the morning's used breakfast dishes. I sat at the kitchen table enjoying a cup of coffee and a blueberry muffin, while Patrick, three months shy of his second birthday, sat nearby in his high chair, still in his yellow-feet Big Bird pajamas. I smiled over at him as he grasped at a Cheerio and lifted it into his mouth. His large hazel eyes drooped a little this morning, as he wasn't sleeping well due to an infection.

The morning light was very pretty as it shone through the bright yellow curtains. Billy Joel's "Everybody Has a Dream" from my all-time favorite album, *The Stranger*, was playing in the background. Patrick and I had been having a nice morning together, and after this midmorning snack, we planned to read one of his Bernstein Bears books. Then it would be naptime.

But when Dave was involved, nothing was pleasant. He walked in without a "hello" or a "good morning," scrutinized the dirty dishes and medical syringe in the sink, and went off on a tirade. "What the hell are the dishes still doing in the sink? Why would you leave the medicine syringe in the sink? What the hell have you been doing all morning?"

I had become so accustomed to this Jekyll-and-Hyde behavior over the previous ten years that I was already prepared for battle. I needed to shield my son from this monster, so I took Patrick out of his highchair, and with my son's arms clung around my neck, I walked to his bedroom to put him in his crib. From previous experience, I should have been expecting the demeaning slap I felt on the back of my head. That always came first. "You are such a slob. You're a no-good mother. You no-good bitch. You're nothing but a piece of shit."

He kicked me from behind as I held our son in my arms. But I was undeterred. I had to get Patrick into his crib. Thankfully, Sarah was in her preschool class. I rushed Patrick into his crib with Dave following on my heels. Patrick usually fell asleep staring at the smiley-faced monkey decal he loved so much. Not this morning. As soon as I let go of him, he stood up and reached his arms out to me, crying.

I turned around, and there was Dave, standing in the middle of Patrick's room. I was trying to make a fast exit into the hall so Patrick wouldn't witness what was about to happen when Dave took two steps toward me and punched me hard in my midsection. I fell back and landed on Sarah's little bed which was adjacent to Patrick's crib. I felt every bit of the solid mighty blow on my five-foot-seven, 120-pound frame. I immediately lost my breath and held onto my stomach in a crunched-up position. I lifted my head and saw Patrick standing in his crib sobbing.

"Get up, you bitch," Dave snarled. I rose from the bed, not because he told me to but because I was ready to fight back, for the first time.

I stood up, holding tightly to my rib cage with both arms crossed, and kicked him as hard as I could. "We were fine until you came home!" I yelled. "I hate you! Get out of here!"

I thought if I left Patrick's room he'd follow, so I turned my back to him and headed towards the door. Then came the second blow. Dave kicked me so hard in my lower back that I landed face down on the carpet.

My back was to Patrick, but I could still hear his sobs. I dreaded that he had to witness this. As I tried to get up, my eyes followed Dave's tan steel-toed construction boot as if in slow motion, and before I could escape its path: *boom*! His boot collided with the right side of my head with such force that my vision faded to total blackness, and then returned in a slow dance of flickering stars. I nearly lost consciousness.

Now Patrick was screaming hysterically. Dave picked him up out of his crib and tried to quiet him, but Patrick was inconsolable, so

Dave put him back down and continued to scream at me and kick me. *Bam*! Another kick to my back knocked me to the floor again. Then he spat in my face and left the room, mumbling, "Fucking bitch. You're worthless."

I managed to get up and limp over to Patrick's crib and pick him up. His ragged breath was now coming in gasps, and I hugged him tightly to my chest. We wept together, and I lay back onto Sarah's bed. Eventually, we both dozed off.

The shame, the humiliation, and the pain of again being beaten up by my husband changed me that day. With my son lying on my chest as we both cried, I made a promise to myself that things would change. I felt a hatred that I had never known in my life. Any love I had for Dave had been completely replaced by sheer repugnance. Staring at the ceiling, I thought, *How will my son view me when he's older if he continues to witness this? Will he think abuse is normal? What kind of man am I raising? What am I teaching my daughter?* That was it. I had to protect my children.

As usual, the next morning there were a dozen red roses on the kitchen table with note. *I'm sorry, I had a bad day at work. Please forgive me. Love, Dave.* I ripped it into pieces and threw it into the trash. He came home later that day and was grumpy as usual. I heard him mumble under his breath—"Well at least there are no dirty dishes in the sink." I'd come to learn that this behavior is common in the cycle of abuse. After abusing me, he'd feel bad, but not about what he had done; he was worried about the possibility of being called out and facing the consequences of his abuse. I eventually came to hate red roses because of what they represented to me.

After that beating, I noticed Patrick's behavior change. He began to cling to my legs more than usual and often held his arms up for me to pick him up whenever Dave was around, but in the days after the recent beating I could barely lift him because of the deep, sharp pains in my chest, arms, back and abdomen. And for days after that attack, it hurt to breathe. Turning my body around to back the car out of the driveway was unbearable. When a few more days passed and the pain wasn't any better, I decided to go to the doctor.

My husband came with me to the doctor's—to make sure I said the right things. After the appointment, the doctor asked to see both of us in his office. He asked what had happened, even though he'd already asked in the exam room. I repeated the story, that I'd injured my rib falling down while roller-skating. That's the lie Dave had come up with. I could sense that doctor knew I was lying, but I didn't change my story. My allegiance to Dave was still strong enough.

As we were about to leave, I went into the bathroom and spotted a poster near the sink that read, DOMESTIC VIOLENCE AWARENESS—ARE YOU BEING ABUSED? I read the diagnostic questions:

1. Does your partner have a bad temper?

2. Do you live in fear of your partner?

3. Has your partner ever physically hurt you?

4. Does it feel like you have to walk on "eggshells" at times so he/she will not explode?

At the time, I didn't think I was being abused, yet I answered yes to all four of the questions. That day a seed was planted. I grabbed a card from underneath the poster and tucked it into my pocket.

A fractured rib, a concussion, and bruises were the physical results of Dave's beating, but the emotional results were much more damaging. As far as Dave was concerned, there was nothing the matter with me—the abuse was "all in my head."

With two small children and very little income to call my own, I felt trapped. I also still dabbled in deluded hope that things would get better and that the physical and verbal abuse might eventually stop. But at least I was starting the climb out of the dark rabbit hole that I had fallen into many years before. I was becoming very, very tired of living in fear.

Every time I picked up Patrick, the pain in my ribs reminded me of the beating that had happened on that cold January day. By the time spring came around, I felt done with my marriage. In my mind, I was finished. The problem was I didn't know how to escape.

We celebrated Patrick's second birthday in April with a birthday party at our home. Because I had no contact with my family, only Dave's family attended. His mother sensed my unhappiness and asked me if anything was wrong. I blurted, "I just don't like the way Dave is treating me these days."

"What do you mean by that? What's he doing?" she asked with a crinkled brow. I underplayed it and said, "Well, he kicked me the other day for nothing."

"His father used to do things like that to me," she said. "But one day I just took a tea kettle and whacked him over the head with it. He never did it again."

I pictured this diminutive Italian woman with a flowered apron tied around her waist cracking her husband over the head with a kettle and thought to myself, *This woman must be crazy. Does she think hitting Dave over the head with a tea kettle is my solution*? I had hoped that she'd become someone I could confide in, that maybe she'd see my pain and help me. I was wrong.

By the time summer rolled around, we had moved into a different house, I was back working part time at Stop and Shop during the evenings and on weekends, and I had just gotten a promotion to the cash office—the happening spot, always a flurry of activity. I was proud of myself. It meant more responsibility, more to learn, and an increase in pay.

For the past year, Dave had tried desperately to get me back under his control. He drove me by a Cape-style home on a quiet residential street that he thought I'd like. "I know you're unhappy, Sue. Let's buy this house. You'll have your privacy back, you can take the kids for walks in the neighborhood, and you'll be happy!" This was something he knew I'd always wanted, a quaint little Cape Cod with room for all of us. I did my best to picture a happy life there. I even got myself to believe that once we moved into the new home Dave would change.

We bought the home and moved in that summer. Of course, nothing changed. Back then, I didn't understand much about abusers, but I later came to learn that the cycle of relationship abuse has four stages: tension building, acute violence, reconciliation or honeymoon, and calm. The cycle continued.

That September, I started back at Springfield Technical Community College taking night classes. When I wasn't working or taking care of the kids, I focused on school. Sarah started kindergarten and dance classes. I enrolled Patrick in a little guppy swimming class. I continued working part time at Stop and Shop, adding weekend shifts to avoid Dave as much as I could. I went out with friends after work.

My friends from Stop and Shop became my saviors during this time. In the presence of these people, I could just be me. I was confident. I liked that person: independent, happy, and free from harm. Free from Dave, free from his constant condescending comments about me and other people. And, free from his control and violence. I longed for more of that.

Any time I spent any money on myself, Dave would call me a selfish bitch, but I didn't care anymore. I shopped for new clothes, and at this point I didn't try to hide them in the trunk of my car. I bought new sunglasses and wore them outside in the yard as I watched the kids play. I could feel myself growing stronger. I was happiest when I was around Sarah and Patrick. Loving them gave me courage. Soon, I stopped wearing my wedding band.

I loved summer nights. I loved the thick, warm air and the quiet. One rare Friday night after work in early July, after the kids went to bed, I opened a bottle of Heineken and went outside to sit in the backyard. Dave came out shortly afterward and sat next to me. "Where's your wedding ring?" he asked.

"I don't wear it anymore," I said.

"Why not?"

"I'm done with this marriage," I replied.

After a long gulp of his beer, he said. "What do you mean by that?"

"Something inside of me has just died, and it's not coming back. I actually grew to love you over the years but not anymore. You're never going to change. You're just a mean person. I've actually come to hate you."

He was silent for a bit and then said, "Well, whether you like it or not, I'm in this marriage until the kids are grown."

"Oh, that's great, we can raise our kids in a toxic atmosphere and let them see us arguing all the time. I'm not going to let them grow up like that." I got up and walked into the house just as Dave spat on the ground.

Our arguments swelled over the next few months, and I started fighting back without backing down. It was getting more and more unbearable for me to be in his company. He was losing control and he knew it. During one incident, I went to the kitchen to grab the phone to call 911—something I had never done before—and he ripped it out of the wall. That's when I knew his fear of being found out was pretty strong. He continued his abusive ways, and I continued not backing down. "Go ahead," I said. "Hit me. Go ahead."

Then, out of the blue, Dave accused me of having an affair.

Because I was so unhappy in the marriage, Dave thought I *must* be having an affair. I think in his mind, he was losing control of me, and he didn't believe that without another man in the wings I'd have the strength or assertiveness to speak my mind or leave him, so he must have assumed that someone was telling me what to do. Like the weeds in our yard, his mean-spiritedness grew. He wouldn't talk to me for days, and when he did it was always condescending. He made fun of my going to school, saying that I'd never get into nursing school—that I'd never amount to anything. His never-ending berating started to make me feel like I was a criminal chained in an interrogation room, and he was trying to break me. Before, his whittling away at my self-esteem always left me feeling like a shadow of the woman I knew I could be. Not anymore. He was not going to break me.

At work, I'd started to confide in my good friend Elaine. We worked together at Stop and Shop most nights, and she was the one I'd go out with after work for a beer. Our favorite place to go was called The Fort. The back side of the bar was lined in colorful ceramic steins from Germany, the booths were cozy, and the beer was good. Elaine was so easy to talk to—she understood and listened. Eventually she became the one I'd reached out to first for help. I started to gather real strength, and more important, I started to feel that I had a new purpose in life: getting out of this miserable marriage.

What lies behind us
And what lies before us
Are tiny matters
Compared to what
Lies within us

—RALPH WALDO EMERSON

CHAPTER 17

JANUARY 1985

*I*t was a blustery cold Saturday in January when I began my escape. Patrick, who would celebrate his third birthday in three months, had been taking a nap on the bottom of the bunk bed he shared with five-year-old Sarah. His cozy warm body was wrapped in his Charlie Brown fleece blanket. Sarah and I had just finished reading an "Arthur" book in the living room. We were fighting colds, so after reading the book, we too laid down for a nap on the sofa.

It was around 4 p.m. when I was jolted awake by the loud bang of the back-door slamming followed by Dave's clunky work boots crossing the kitchen floor and heading towards me. He'd been out drinking at an Italian American club with his father, which he did most Saturday afternoons. He smelled of garlic and beer as he entered the small living room. With his winter coat still on, he said, "What are you doing sleeping? It's the middle of the day." The minute I saw him, I thought: *Oh God, here we go again. He's totally looking to fight.*

"I wasn't feeling well, and neither was Sarah, so we were napping," I replied.

"What's for dinner?" he bellowed. Why haven't you started dinner?"

I got up from the sofa and placed Sarah back down, still sleeping, and covered her up with a blanket. As I entered the kitchen, Dave slapped me on the side of my head, grabbed my long ponytail, and yanked me down onto the floor with it. Kicking me toward the back door, he shouted, "You lazy bitch. You're never going to amount to anything. You're a piece of white trash. Your family is white trash. Just get out of this house, nobody wants you here."

As I kicked back at him, his hand gripped my ponytail tighter and dragged me with it the rest of the way, opened the door and threw me out onto the screened-in porch. He slammed the door behind him, which shattered one of the small windowpanes and left broken glass all around me. "Leave the house," he said. "You white trash bitch."

"I am not leaving my kids with you—you're sick," I retorted. "Why don't you leave? We were happy until you came home."

"You will *never* get my kids," he said. "I will kill you if you ever leave with my kids. I will hunt you down, kill you, and then I'll go after your whole fucking family and kill them too. Nobody will miss you."

It was about twenty degrees out on the porch. I stepped lightly in my socks, trying to avoid the broken glass, and yelled, "Let me in!" Sarah was awake, and through the broken window I could see her crying. She pleaded, "Daddy, let her in." I did not see or hear Patrick but was sure that he was awake by now. I kept banging on the door. "Let me in. I am not leaving without my kids!"

Ten freezing minutes later, he opened the door. I ran to Sarah, picked her up and carried her into Patrick's room where my little boy was now hiding in his closet. I hugged them both and said, "It's ok. Try not to be scared. Just stay in here until I come to get you."

I dashed into my bedroom, and Dave followed. As I sat on the side of the bed crying, he picked up my winter ankle boot and threw it across the room. I had no time to duck, and it smacked me directly on the nose. Then he charged me and punched me in the face and the stomach. I yelled, "I hate you . . . I hate you . . . I hate you."

"I'm not stopping until you get the fuck out of this house!" he shouted. "Nobody wants you here. Get the fuck out."

"Leave me alone!" I shouted back. "I am *never* leaving this house without my kids!" I ran into the kitchen to try to call the police. Dave caught up, yanked the phone out of the wall, and threw it onto the floor. I ran back to my bedroom. Dave followed, shoved me back onto the bed, and like a cowboy mounting a horse, straddled my hips with his knees, and gripped my neck with his large calloused hands. His face turned apple-red with rage, and his grip became tighter and tighter as I fought back. I reached for his face and kicked and punched whatever was in my reach. As my lungs burned from lack of air, I saw dark spots across my vision. Slowly the world started to fade. I felt my arms go limp. Only darkness. *Did I die?* All of a sudden, I gasped for air. I got off the bed and ran into the kids' room and closed the door behind me. We hugged, and I pretended that I was ok. Then I heard Dave leave the house and drive away.

The kids and I fell asleep on their bottom bunk. An hour later, I awoke and put Sarah to sleep up on her bed and then went into the bathroom to assess the damage. My nose was tilted slightly to the left and the bridge was starting to turn purple. My two front teeth were chipped. I wasn't a nurse yet, but I knew what a concussion felt like. This headache was just like the times before. I knew that this was the turning point. I needed help. *I have to get out before he kills me.*

I lay in my bed, trying to rest my throbbing head, but now my thoughts were racing. I began to plan, and during the process of my thinking through the first steps to escape, I began to feel a calmness come over me. I felt as if God was speaking to me. *You will be all right, just listen and I will show you the way. Follow me, Susan, and I will lead you to safety.*

Dave came home and slipped quietly into bed next to me. He smelled of beer. I lay there frozen, thinking about all I'd have to do to escape, and when I awoke the next morning, I felt reenergized. I dressed for work. Dave took the kids to get donuts and then to his parents' house for lunch. I saw that he'd left me one of his "love notes" on the kitchen counter. This one read, "You are a piece of shit and will never amount to anything." I ripped it into pieces and threw it into the trash.

I called my friend and Stop and Stop boss, Katie. She was working the morning shift and would go off when I came in at 12 p.m. She was a role model for me, and I knew I could trust her. I told her all about the abuse, admitting that it wasn't the first time. I didn't want to go into work looking beaten up, so we made a plan: she would cover my shift, and if Dave called looking for me, she would tell him I was busy and couldn't talk. So that afternoon, instead of working the 12–6 pm shift, I drove to Stop and Shop, parked my car, and left it there.

The East Coast was in the middle of a cold wave, and the temperature was in the single digits that day. Katie and Erin, another work friend, met me in the parking lot, where we sat in Erin's car and planned my escape. They both greeted me with a hug, their mouths opened wide and eyes filled with tears and fury when they saw my face.

Katie went back into work, and Erin I drove to a gas station where I found a pay phone with a phone book and started scribbling the numbers of women's shelters and domestic abuse hotlines. I took out the tattered card I had taken from my doctor's office and dialed the phone number for an abuse–rape crisis hotline. The woman who answered asked if I needed a place to stay. I told her I had to go home that night to get my children. And so began our planning. I would leave Dave the following day.

That night I sat with Sarah and Patrick and watched the Disney Sunday-night movie. Dave sat near us and wasn't speaking to me. I thought, *Guess what, asshole? Tomorrow we're outta here.* After the movie was over, I read Sarah and Patrick a bedtime story, gave them both a good night hug and kiss, and prepared myself for bed. My stomach was a nervous mix of excitement and relief. I was praying that the next day would go as planned, but that night I was still going to be sleeping next to a violent man, so I went into the kitchen and grabbed a large carving knife. I tucked it under a kitchen dishtowel, carried it into my bedroom, and slid it under my mattress.

Monday morning arrived. At the sound of my husband's car revving up, I jumped out of bed and ran into the living room. It was 6:30 on a dark, cold morning as I watched the rusted-out '67 Volvo crawl down the snow-lined street. Out loud, I said, "You'll never lay another fucking hand on me."

I scrambled around, gathering clothes and toys for the kids, plus snacks, toiletries, and the bank book. I woke the kids up, sat them down on my bed, and knelt on the floor in front of them. I looked deeply into their eyes and said, "You need to listen to me very carefully. Momma is going to do something today to keep you safe. I'm not going to live with your father anymore because he hurts me, and that's not right. I love you so much, and I don't want you to be scared." Patrick at almost three years old reacted with quiet, which was not unlike him. Sarah cried; she understood a little more as she was three years older. She said, "You mean Daddy isn't going to be living with us anymore?"

I said, "That's right, sweetie, he's not." I hugged them tightly and started packing the car. I dropped Sarah off at her kindergarten class and walked to the front office where I told the woman at the front desk that I was obtaining a restraining order against my husband that day and that I was the only one allowed to pick Sarah up from this school, ever. Her mouth dropped open. I ran into my friend Mary in the parking lot and told her the ugly story. She offered to take care of Patrick as I ran around that morning taking care of more details—an offer I gratefully accepted.

I drove to the restaurant where Christine, the woman I'd spoken to on the phone, had asked me to meet her. We sat across from each other in a booth. I still had a headache and had been fighting nausea since the previous day. I ordered a Coke. She drank black coffee. Her long blond hair was parted down the middle and covered the front of her flowered blouse. Like an angel, Christine had bright blue eyes that sparkled with hope. She was a full-time psychologist, and she volunteered part-time at the YWCA as a legal advocate for abused women. We talked about where I was going to stay (at my friend Katie's house), how I would go about getting a restraining order (go to the courthouse and request one), and how to survive the next few days (any way I could). She could not accompany me to court that day because of a prior commitment but told me where to go and what to ask for.

I drove to the courthouse and made my way to a clerk. The middle-aged, heavyset brunette woman saw my bruised face, then quickly looked back down at her papers.

"May I help you?"

"Could I please have a 209-A form?" I asked.

"Do you want to file a complaint for protection from abuse?"

"Yes. Does it include a restraining order?" I asked.

"Do you have legal representation?"

"No, I do not."

She handed me a two-page form. "This form has everything you need on it," she replied and told me to fill it out and bring it back to her. I filled out the necessary paperwork, returned it to the clerk, and then sat for an hour on a wooden bench that looked like a church pew. Then my name was called to speak to the judge.

"Do you have legal representation here today?" he asked.

"No, Your Honor, I do not. I met with a legal advocate and she could not be with me today, but she told me what to do," I replied.

He paused, carefully looking at my face. "Did your husband do that to you?"

"Yes, Your Honor, he did."

"Is this the first time he has done something like this to you?" he asked.

"No, Your Honor, it is not."

"Are you afraid for your safety?"

"Yes, Your Honor I am, and for my children."

"Does he own any weapons?" he inquired.

"Not that I know of," I responded.

The judge granted me a temporary restraining order and physical custody of my children. Dave would have to vacate our home and stay at least fifty feet away from me. I walked to my car so happy and proud of myself that I felt like waving the paper and screaming, "I did it! You can't hurt me anymore!"

The police department was the next stop on the journey I had just begun. To make sure there was no confusion and to be assured that the police actually received the restraining order, I hand-delivered a copy to them. Now it was up to them to serve my husband with the order. I picked Sarah up at school, stopped at my friend's to pick up Patrick, and then headed to my friend Katie's for the night. I pulled my car into the garage to hide it from view.

I felt relief for finally opening up about the dark, secret part of my life. And I felt pride for having taken action against my abuser. But I knew that once Dave found out what I'd done, he'd be like a wild animal looking for blood.

My friends from Stop and Shop put their lives on hold to help me survive for over a week during that winter of 1985. The first night, my friend Katie and her husband Steve gave up their king-size heated waterbed for the three of us to sleep in. The comfort and safety my bruised and shivering body felt that first night will be forever in my soul. I curled up in the warmth of my children and awoke to a new day. But long-term comfort wasn't going to be in our cards for some time.

That week, Sarah didn't go to school, and I didn't go to work. For the next five days, we hid out at the house of Lana, another friend of mine from Stop and Shop. She lived in a town about a half hour away, and I knew Dave would never look there. He didn't even know these friends of mine existed. My friend Lana knew a friend who knew a good lawyer, and I met with him to discuss my options before going back to court. He eventually became my divorce attorney.

The court had scheduled a hearing seven days later to determine whether the temporary order should be continued. I needed to be present in court on that day in order for that to happen, so one week after my first visit to court, I was in court again, this time with my soon-to-be ex-husband sitting nearby. He approached me in the hallway and tried to get me back under his thumb.

"Sue, what are you doing?" he said. Have you lost your mind?" I didn't answer. "Can we go to the end of the hallway to talk?" he asked.

"No, you're never going to lay a hand on me again. This is what I'm doing."

This time Christine, the legal advocate, was with me, and she did all the talking. The restraining order was renewed for six months, and temporary physical custody of my children was awarded to me.

After calling the police department to make sure Dave had vacated the house, I returned home with Sarah and Patrick. I was frightened to go home alone, but I declined an offer from the police to have an escort. Erin went with me, and when we entered the house, the first thing we checked was his closet. Most of his things were gone. Erin stayed with me for a few nights, and then I was on my own. Knowing that Dave wasn't allowed to ever set foot in here again brought a smile to my face. I had all the locks changed, and I started to feel safe, a sensation I hadn't experienced in a very long time.

CHAPTER 18

JANUARY 1986

*I*t was a little before midnight on New Year's Eve when I awoke to blackness. I lay on my sofa covered in two fuzzy blankets, with a dried-up washcloth on my forehead. I glanced over at the side window in the living room and saw that the snow was starting to accumulate. The nearby streetlight caused the ice crystals on the window to sparkle like silver glitter. I smiled. I'd always loved a good snowstorm.

It had been one year since I'd left my abusive husband. As my body continued shaking from the feverish chill, I turned on the television set to watch the ball drop in Times Square. The New Year had arrived. I'd been sick with the flu for about a week and felt depressed at the same time. I awoke to a new year—one filled with new possibilities. How was I going to start anew? A new beginning, that's just what I needed. Good-bye 1985, hello 1986.

I'd been attending Monday night support group meetings at the battered women's shelter, often with Sarah and Patrick in tow. With other children, they were watched by a volunteer for the hour-and-a-half meeting time. This place opened my eyes to a world I'd never imagined, a pained and tragic world where the bruised and battered turned to feel safe. But the women in the group exuded hope.

Supporting my children and myself was my first priority. I wanted and needed financial independence. I didn't want to be a part-time cashier at Stop and Shop for the rest of my life; I wanted a career. Years earlier, I had thought of becoming a nurse, and the idea was never far from my mind, but I'd never believed I was smart enough. I was different now, stronger. My soul was guiding me, and I was ready for a big change.

That New Year's morning was a typical January day, bringing with it an after-a-New-England-blizzard kind of calm. The streets were quiet, the sun was blinding against the snow, and the noise of snowplows rumbled in the distance. Four-foot snowdrifts covered the streets. Although the temperature outside was below freezing, my heart felt warm. I was starting to feel the wonderful comfort that comes when you know exactly what you need to do. And I felt the empowerment that comes from knowing that you *are* going to do it. I was going to become a nurse.

I began researching the requirements for admission to local nursing schools. The following month I applied to the nearby Baystate Medical Center School of Nursing and was accepted into the three-year RN diploma program. I was thirty years old. Sarah and Patrick were six and four.

We celebrated my acceptance by going out to dinner at Sarah's and Patrick's favorite restaurant, the Hu Ke Lau. We ate Chinese food and talked about our new life while watching the fire and hula dancers. My job at Stop and Shop was part-time, so they were used to my being around much more than a full-time schedule would require. We talked about the challenges the next three years would bring. I told them I'd need their help to get through, and they agreed happily, especially to the part about my buying them new bikes when I finished.

They had visitation with their father on Wednesday evenings and every other weekend, and it was confusing for them. He often told them, "I still love your mom, and I don't know why she left me," and he asked them to report that thought to me. In contrast, I kept the message to them consistent: "No matter what your father says, we will never be back together. I am sorry he is confusing you."

For over a year at that point, both Dave's lawyer and mine had been working on a divorce settlement. We had previously agreed on a visitation schedule, and that remained intact. As far as assets went, we were both owners of the two houses: the two-family home and a small Cape, plus two cars. As much as I hated the two-family home, my lawyer suggested that I ask for it in the settlement because in the long run it would be worth more. He was right. I asked for and got the two-family house, and although I needed to take out a loan to attend school, I was able to rent out one floor and live on the other. The amount I collected in rent covered my monthly mortgage payment. Dave was paying child support every two weeks, and with my paycheck from my part-time job, there was enough to get me through. Dave moved into the other house and we each kept a car.

The divorce was finalized just before summer, and by August the kids and I had moved into the two-family house. I started nursing school in the fall. The first year was an adjustment for all of us. But I knew if I could just stick it out, all the sacrifice and work would pay off. Within weeks of the first day of classes, people started dropping out. But rather than let that discourage me, I became more determined to make this work, no matter how hard it got.

After the first year of nursing school, I was eligible to enter the Student Nurse Assistant Program. It was designed to help nursing students learn more by working in the field, and we'd be able to put to use the skills we'd already learned in school. I took a position on a trauma floor and was both scared and invigorated by the challenges that I knew lay ahead. Letting go of my job at Stop and Shop involved a bittersweet good-bye. I knew that I'd truly miss the friends I'd made while working there, and I left filled with gratitude to every one of them for helping me in my time of need.

During my second year of nursing school, I found a mentor in Jean, one of my instructors. When I entered her office one Friday afternoon during winter finals, she said a bright, "Hi, Sue, come on in."

Sitting at her desk, Jean was neatly dressed in a pressed white nurse's uniform, her graduation pin from Boston College prominently pinned on one lapel. She wore a nurse's uniform only on the clinical days she taught students on the nursing floors in the hospital. She'd shared with me previously that she'd graduated from the nursing program at Boston College twenty years earlier. She'd now been teaching for five years and had been working in the hospital for fifteen. She wore no makeup on her oval face, which showed off her peaches-and-cream complexion. Her ash-brown hair was pulled back into a short bun and, as she always did, she looked up at me from her desk with a gentle kind smile through her gold, wire-rimmed glasses.

"Jean, I don't know if I can do this anymore," I said.

I was struggling with the math class that I'd been taking. I was waking up at 4 o'clock almost every morning, worried that I wouldn't pass the final exam.

"Do what?" she asked.

"The classes, the tests, the papers due, all the reading—it's overwhelming me. I just can't do it all."

"Try to look at the big picture," she told me. "You've come so far. It's just one more exam. You'll get through it."

At the time I couldn't share her breezy optimism. My GPA hinged on passing this test, and told her how much I hated math.

"I have a great book that I've lent out before and that may help you," she said.

She got up from her desk, walked over to a bookcase, and pulled out a large paperback that said *Math for Nurses* in bold red letters across the front.

"This book," she said, "explains math in a much simpler way. It has a lot of visuals in it. Try to review the parts you think you need help with, and then study as much as you can over the weekend."

"But what happens if I don't pass?"

"Try not to overthink it, Sue. You tend to do that." She glanced at me with a smile and said, "I have faith in you. Just give it your best shot. That's all you can do."

Just her saying that made me feel better. Over the next year and a half, Jean became the encouraging mother figure I needed. Her constant support kept my spirit alive.

I took the exam on a Monday afternoon. It was over in about an hour, and I let out a big sigh of relief as I walked out of the classroom. Then on Tuesday morning I received the results. With a smile that stretched from cheek to cheek, I knocked on Jean's office door.

"I passed!" I said with pride. I had needed a score of at least seventy-eight to pass the test, and I'd gotten a seventy-nine.

"I'm so happy for you. I knew you could do it!"

I walked out of her office with my head held high and the feeling that nothing would ever get in my way. With her support, I felt unstoppable.

The following spring semester, I started clinical rotations for "community nursing." This included mental health nursing and spending time in local hospitals that offered psychiatric care. One of my clinical rotations for psychiatric nursing was at Northampton State Hospital, the same mental hospital where my sister Marie had been admitted. This place had had a huge impact on me many years earlier and to see it again now, brought me back to time and place that I'd rather have forgotten. Little had changed since my first visit there twelve years earlier. The smell of pine and body odor hung heavily in the air, and the place still gave me the creeps. As a student nurse taking care of these patients, I had a different perspective than a visitor. The nurses showed empathy for the patients, which made me think about Marie and her illness. I wondered where she was living now and how she was doing.

The following day I visited the detox center where my father had spent more than one stint. I spoke with the nurse and told her that my father had been a patient there. She asked me his name and after I told her, she seemed acutely focused on my every word. She told me he'd stayed there a number of times, and added, "Such a nice guy. It's too bad he never got better." I was taken aback when she admitted that she had known him back in high school and that back then they'd dated for a while. "Until he met your mother," she added.

A few weeks later, I began to have trouble swallowing. When I'd try to eat anything, I was afraid I'd choke on it and die. I was unable to concentrate, felt sick to my stomach most days, and was convinced something terrible was the matter with me, that I had some type of life-threatening illness. I was afraid to be alone, I became sleep deprived, and it took all my energy to keep all the parts of my life intact.

It was the same feeling I'd had when I was a teenager and told my mom I thought I was going crazy. But this time the feeling was more intense. My anxiety had graduated to panic attacks, and I felt enveloped by a sense of impending doom. It was as if a big black cloud was hovering above me, just waiting for the right time to launch a deadly lightning bolt. I thought, *This is it, it's finally happening. I'm going crazy like my sister.*

Although I might have looked fine on the outside, inside I was falling apart. One night I awoke in the middle of the night, unable to catch my breath and felt certain I was dying. I made it through the night and then reached out to a friend at work who suggested I go to the employee health office. I was worried about my kids as much as I was worried about myself, so I accepted her advice.

After talking with Chris, a social worker, for close to an hour, I felt much better. She knew the right questions to ask and deciphered enough of my story to suggest a cause of my anxiety: my dysfunctional upbringing. She gave me books to read: *Adult Children of Alcoholics*, by Janet Woititz, *It Will Never Happen to Me!—Children of Alcoholics As Youngsters—Adolescents—Adults*, by Claudia Black, and *After the Tears—Helping Children of Alcoholics Heal Their Childhood Trauma*, by Jane Middleton-Moz and Lorie Dwinell. She also gave me cards with recommendations for a few therapists in the area.

The following morning happened to be a Saturday. I was grateful that Sarah and Patrick were at their dad's. After pacing around my bedroom for about ten minutes, I sat on the edge of my bed and picked up the phone that sat on my bedside table. I dialed the number of the first therapist that Chris had given me. When a voice message came on, I hung up, took a deep breath, and dialed the other number. A woman named Cindy answered. "Why do you want to see a therapist?" she asked me.

I couldn't answer. Instead, only large gasps and sobs came through over the phone. Through the sobs, I eventually choked out the words, "I'm having a lot of anxiety and I need help." We made an appointment for two days later. After I hung up, I dropped onto my bed, face first and cried into my pillow until I had no more tears left.

As soon as I started seeing Cindy, a new world had opened up to me. My weekly visits opened my unconscious. Like the opening of floodgates, the memories I'd kept hidden for so long came rushing out at breakneck speed. And I found it fascinating that despite my emotional gushing and the mental exhaustion that followed, the result of my therapy was that my anxiety settled down. What I didn't know at the time was that Cindy would become a true confidante in my life for over twenty-five years as my therapist. Through the years I saw her as often or as little as I needed her. She was and is one of my life's greatest gifts and the one who got me through the toughest times.

The Adult Children of Alcoholics meetings I started attending on Wednesday evenings replaced my meetings at the battered women's support group. Sarah and Patrick stayed home, watched by a babysitter. I sat quiet most nights, mesmerized by the idea that so many people could have experienced the same kind of neglect and abuse that I had. Their stories were haunting. I felt solidarity with them and began to understand that I possessed many characteristics of an adult child of an alcoholic. I lacked the spontaneity of other kids my age due to the undercurrent of tension and anxiety that was omnipresent in my house. I was withdrawn and couldn't be carefree because I was always on guard about what might happen next. I kept most of my feelings to myself and lived on a steady diet of hope. I always hoped that I'd walk into my home one day and everything would be fine, that I'd just been having one long nightmare.

I continued to read books from many well-known authors on the subjects of abuse, alcoholism, and codependency. They became my connection to understanding my past and my lifeline to hope. A daily meditation book sat at my bedside, and I read it every morning and night. I started to recognize the patterns of past abuse and neglect and began to understand why I'd made the choices I had. And I began to feel less alone.

A few months after my initial visit with Cindy, I began my final year of nursing school. During my rotation in the Intensive Care Unit at Baystate Medical Center, I spotted a tall, dark-haired, good looking guy across the busy corridor. The droning beep of cardiac monitors echoed in the hall, and the air sat thick with the silence of patients getting ready to pass on or fight to give life another try. Their loved ones wandered in circles. Doctors dressed in pale green scrubs and operating room caps sped along the hallways as beads of sweat dotted their brows. Nurses dressed in identical colored scrubs entered and left their patients' cubicles.

Dressed in my white-and-teal nursing uniform with the BMC logo on the front, I looked up to see the dark-haired doctor approaching me. I was pretty sure he was a resident because of his green scrubs.

I noticed that my new digital watch wasn't showing the correct time, so I unbuckled it to reset the time. While I was going through the settings on my watch, the resident approached me and playfully tossed me a small foam ball. "Catch," he said, his face lighting up with a smile when I caught it. There was nothing shy about this man, so confident and playful as he sauntered over and introduced himself. I was a little intimated by his playfulness, but I smiled back and tried to be subtle as I checked him out. His eyes were Caribbean-blue, and his black hair was short on top with long-ish curls in the back. He had a matching mustache and stood about six feet two. I'd always had a thing for tall men with curly hair. I noticed his watch was tied into the waistband of his scrubs. He introduced himself as Bruce and said he was from Los Angeles.

Bruce asked me what I was trying to do. When I told him I was having difficulty figuring out how to change the time on my new digital watch, he said, "I can do it for you if you like. I just changed mine." I handed him my watch, and we chatted while he worked on it.

"Are you in nursing school?" he asked nonchalantly.

"Yes," I said. "I'll be graduating in three months."

"What school do you go to?"

"Here, Baystate Medical Center."

"Do you get a bachelor's degree when you graduate?" he asked.

"No," I told him. "This is a three-year diploma, hospital-based training program. I'll have to go on if I want to get my bachelor's degree. I'll do that eventually, but right now I just want to graduate and start working. I'm a little burned out from school."

"My mom's a nurse," he said. "She works in L.A. as a discharge planner. I think she went to a diploma nursing school, too." He finished my watch, handed it back to me, and said, "All set, there you go."

The conversation lasted only a few minutes, but it made a long-lasting impression on me. I was instantly smitten.

Over the next few months, I'd see Bruce walking the halls of the hospital here and there, and we'd acknowledge each other with a quick "Hi." I wondered what his medical specialty was, but I didn't have the nerve to ask him.

I graduated in May of 1989. My mother and my sisters came to my graduation. My mom hugged me and told me she was proud of me. Sarah and Patrick handed me a bouquet of flowers. My sister

Joan threw me a party. I was on top of the world. My head spun with excitement. I'd never had a graduation party from high school, so this was extra special for me, and Joan knew that. I felt like I was floating on a white puffy cloud—the kind my sisters and I had gazed at for long summer hours, trying to make out images as we lay on the green grass in the field across from our home.

It had been almost five years since that terrifying weekend when I'd somehow conjured the courage to leave my abusive husband and start a new life for my children and myself. I had dreamed of a new life, and now I had it. My life was happy as a single mom. My kids were my world. I wanted to stay in that moment forever and freeze this feeling that I had ached for most of my life. For once I was happy and able to feel it.

Although my ex-husband was always trying to disturb my happiness and the rhythm of my life without him, I tried not to be fazed by it. Through our attorneys, we had set up a schedule for when the kids would spend time with him, and we stuck to that. He was living in our old house. Other than when I dropped the kids off, I hardly saw him, and I liked it that way.

The weekend after my graduation was Dave's weekend to have the kids. I pulled up to the curb at his home and there he was, waiting outside. He walked over to the driver's side of my car, looked down at my new sneakers, and said, "Living high off the hog, I see. We'll see how long that lasts."

It took everything I had to be civil to him in front of the kids. I pretended I was wearing body armor, so anything he said would just bounce off me.

Six weeks after graduation, I found out that I'd passed my written boards and was now an official RN. In June, I accepted a full-time nursing position in the labor and delivery unit at Baystate Medical Center, my dream job.

In July, two months after graduating from nursing school, I

started my twelve-week orientation as a registered nurse on the labor and delivery unit. A few weeks into orientation, I peered through the heavy glass window of operating room number one and noticed someone staring back at me through a set of clear-colored OR goggles. My stomach flip-flopped. I thought it looked like that resident, Bruce, whom I had met in the ICU. Could it be? What would he be doing here? I'd noticed some white lab coats hanging on hooks nearby, so I glanced down to see if his was one of them. There it was. The hospital name badge hung low on the front pocket of his white lab coat. Dr. Bruce Morris. I found out that he was an intern and was in his first year of a four-year OB/GYN residency program. *Wow*, I thought, *what a coincidence.*

From then on, whenever I saw him, I felt butterflies in my stomach.

My lawyer had been right about my real estate options. I sold the two-family for a good profit, and the proceeds enabled me to buy a brand-spanking new car for the first time in my life: a gray, four-door Honda Accord. Delighted about finally finishing school, I viewed it as a gift to myself.

During that summer, I looked around for homes that I'd be able to afford. I'd always wanted to live in a smaller town and had my eye on a town known for its quaintness and good schools. Late that summer, I purchased the house of my dreams, a blue, two-bedroom Cape Cod with white shutters on a quiet street in the dreamy town of East Longmeadow, Massachusetts. I finally said good-bye to the two-family house and never looked back. Sarah and Patrick—who were now eight and ten years old—and I moved into our new home in late August, right before the start of the school year.

The doom and anxiety I had been working through with Cindy had settled down, and I decided to pause my weekly sessions with her. She sent me a beautiful flower arrangement with a lovely note attached to mark the occasion.

I drove around exploring my new town on my days off, enjoying the winding roads and lovely views of the many farms along Porter Road and Route 83 that led into Connecticut. I rolled down my car windows and stopped to take pictures and smell the fresh fall air. I loved the safety and quaintness I felt here. East Longmeadow became my haven.

The first night in our new home, Sarah and Patrick and I slept together in my queen-sized bed, Sarah's head on one of my shoulders, Patrick's on the other. The house we'd lived in before was on a busy road with a traffic light right in front and was always noisy. But here, I woke up in the middle of the night from the quiet, loving the feeling of being curled up with the warmth of my children. We were cozy and safe, what a contrast to just five years earlier. I wanted to stay here forever.

Sarah and Patrick started new schools, and we bought pumpkins for our new home and placed them on the front steps. Then we hung a fall wreath on the front door and quickly settled in. I was proud of my new home and of myself. For once, the train ride of my life was moving smoothly along the rails.

In September, I completed my orientation to the labor and delivery unit and started working three twelve-hour night shifts per week. Bruce and I worked in the same area, so we ran into each other here and there. Every time I spoke with him, I learned something new. I loved the reflection I got of myself through his eyes. He was laid back, and I really liked that about him. I figured it was because he was from California. He had a good relationship with his parents, spoke fondly of his mother, and was just an upfront guy—confident, almost cocky. As I started my shift at seven in the evening, he'd be going off his shift. I loved that he always stopped by the room I was in just to say good-bye.

At work one December evening, the nurses and residents were sitting around the nurses' station chatting about Christmas parties that were on the horizon. I loved Christmas time, and for me that meant a real Christmas tree. I mentioned wanting one for my new house this year. Bruce offered to come with me to chop down a tree at my favorite tree farm in Connecticut, right over the East Longmeadow border. In return I'd make him breakfast. It was a deal.

The following week, shortly after I saw Sarah and Patrick off on the bus, Bruce arrived at my house. I made him breakfast as I'd promised, and then we headed out to Pell Farm to get a tree. After choosing one that I liked, he cut it down and secured it on top of my car. Then we drove back to my house where he helped me put it into the tree stand. The decorating would be saved for later when the kids got home from school. That Christmas Day, I stood at the kitchen window in our new home and watched Sarah and Patrick as they made snow angels in the backyard. My heart was at peace.

After Christmas, Bruce and I became fast friends, and I started spending more time with him. I'd been happy living by myself but being around him stirred up thoughts of my future. A part of me was worried, though. I wasn't ready for a romantic relationship; it just seemed like an entanglement to me. I didn't want any complications. But we continued to spend time together, and slowly the emotional barriers I had built up for so long started to come down. The love and safety I felt with Bruce was a dramatic contrast to the constant insecurity and fear I'd felt with Dave.

In January, we celebrated Bruce's birthday. Our friendship just naturally became a courtship, and by March, we were a couple. Over the next few months, Bruce got to know Sarah and Patrick, and, with my approval, even bought them a dog that Patrick named "Fang." I was happy as a lark when I was around Bruce and thought, *Do I dare to dream*? I was falling in love and started to envision a life with him in it.

Love was in the air that spring as we both started to talk about the future. As corny as it sounds, we started out as friends and ended up as lovers. Then we took a lovely trip to Jamaica together. In addition to it being the first time I'd ever flown, it was also the first time I'd left my kids for more than a few days. I'd been so used to playing the mom role for the previous several years that it was delightful to feel like a woman in love.

During that summer, we visited Bruce's family in Los Angeles with Sarah and Patrick in tow. That's when I became keenly aware that Bruce was the one I was supposed to spend the rest of my life with. I began to trust again. Still, intimacy was an issue for me. The wall I had built over the years that had encircled me for protection was now a barrier to intimacy. Over time, I'd become used to that wall, and it had served me well. But I didn't need it anymore. It was an obstacle to moving forward in my life with Bruce, and I wanted it gone. I reentered therapy and worked hard to understand and eliminate my internal resistance to intimacy. Slowly the wall came crumbling down and my heart opened to love.

I never thought I'd have a relationship in which I felt like an equal partner and where I felt safe and loved unconditionally. With Bruce, there was no arguing or belittling, and best of all, no yelling. I used to dream about this type of happiness and wonder what it would feel like. Now I knew.

Bruce and I married the following October, in 1991. We exchanged our wedding vows at First Church in Longmeadow, the same the church where I'd spent so many Monday nights attending ACOA meetings, the place where I'd learned so much about my past and myself. As I walked down the aisle with Sarah and Patrick, I thought of how far I'd come. Never in my wildest dreams did I think I'd be here.

My mom and dad, all of my sisters, and my brother attended the wedding. I made sure to tell the band that I didn't want a father–daughter dance. I was still in the beginning stages of reconnecting with my father and didn't want either of us to feel awkward. But someone dropped the ball because all of a sudden at the reception I heard, "It is now time for the father–daughter dance." My dad stood up quickly and walked to the dance floor. He looked so proud and nervous standing out on there that I joined him and danced to "Daddy's Little Girl."

Somehow during this dance, my relationship with my father seemed to change. He hugged me close and whispered in my ear an apology for not being the father he should have been. I cried. He'd never held me like this before, so soft and tender. The hole in my heart healed over that day. I wouldn't have believed it, but I felt an empathy toward him that I hadn't experienced before. Still, I wasn't sure I wanted him in my life. It pained me too much to see him like this, battered by alcohol abuse, so I decided to take it slowly.

His once-chiseled facial features were now hidden behind a puffiness and a riddling of sun spots. His eyes were bloodshot and his belly distended. His heavy hooded eyes lacked the luster and oomph that I'd seen in him when he was younger, and their whites were reddish and tinged with yellow. His posture slumped slightly as if he carried the troubles of the world on his shoulders. The smell of beer, cigarettes, and cologne encircled him as his labored breathing wheezed from years of smoking. I wanted my old dad back, but when I looked into his eyes, I knew that man was gone.

After the honeymoon, I visited my father at his home. I even brought Sarah and Patrick with me. I tried to ignore the filthy kitchen with dishes filling the sink, the rusty pipes and stained toilet, the smoky bedroom littered with cigarette butts, and the stained pajamas. I just tried to see my dad. I intuitively knew that the love he had for me had been there all along. What I didn't know was that my father would pass away four months later.

Bruce and I had a daughter two and a half years after our wedding. We named her Samantha. We became a family of five and bought a larger home, a three-thousand-square-foot colonial with ten rooms, four bedrooms, four baths, and a great backyard in East Longmeadow, and for the next twelve years, we lived there as a family.

I didn't yet know that Samantha would become the perfect mixture of Bruce and me. Or how very different and rewarding it would be to raise a child when both parents respect each other. Or that Bruce and I would reach the milestone of twenty-six years of marriage and travel to places like Hawaii, Paris, Switzerland, and London. Nor could I have fathomed the way that breast cancer would change my life in the years to come.

CHAPTER 19

2013–2015

*T*he EMDR treatments seemed to work because emotionally I was feeling like myself again. I had the time to focus on my physical health, so I started doing yoga regularly and found a trainer. Samantha and I established "Tea Time." When she'd get home from school, we'd spend a half hour catching up while having a snack of cookies or banana bread and tea. In the cool months, it was hot chocolate or hot tea, and in the warm months, iced tea.

Life had rolled on. Patrick and Emily married, and during our mother–son dance, he said, "Mom thank you for making me the man I am today." It brought tears to my eyes. I looked up at my son, six feet two, dark haired, and handsome, and marveled at how much he looked like a healthy, young version of my father.

Samantha had graduated from high school and was ready to start the second semester of her sophomore at the University of Denver. I continued my yearly visits with my oncologist and was now off the anti-estrogen drug I had been taking for five years. I was enjoying life not working in nursing. It gave me the opportunity to travel when I wanted. I was grateful to be able to visit my grandbabies whenever I wanted and to be able to regularly check in on my mom.

One winter's day, I was feeling especially contented, sitting yoga style on the deep brown tapestry sofa in my living room. Snow had been falling all morning, pretty untypical for St. Louis. But I loved it. A fire glowed in front of me, and my favorite radio station was playing smooth jazz softly in the background. I was enjoying my second cup of coffee and reading the Sunday *New York Times* when my cell phone vibrated next to me. It was my brother, Charles. "Mom looks like she's lost some weight, and she seems frailer to me," he said. Charles also noted that at times she seemed confused. He was worried that one day he'd show up at her house and she'd be on the floor from an accidental fall. He had recently placed a safety grip in the shower but was worried about the stairs that led up to her bedroom and down to the basement where her washer and dryer were located. He'd already placed extra railings on both sets of stairs, and he wasn't sure what more he could do to minimize her risk of falling.

The quaint town of Dennis, Massachusetts, where my mom lived, was having one of its worst winters in decades. Charles also lived on the Cape, a short fifteen-minute drive away from Mom. As the sibling who lived the closest, he checked in on her regularly. The past month's recent snowstorms had left my eighty-three-year-old mother stranded in her home for a couple of days at a time. She even lost power for an entire weekend. Charles was becoming increasingly concerned.

My mom and Charles shared a very close relationship. Partly, I think, because he's the only boy in our family of seven kids, but he also lived the closest to her for the longest time. We regularly teased him that he was Mom's favorite. All six of us girls had dark brown hair and dark eyes, while Charles was born with blond hair and blue eyes. He was a very cute kid—another thing we teased him about. Mom loved the fact that he lived nearby and that she and Charles had a breakfast date once a week.

Charles's work had been taking him out of town lately for a few days at a time, and he was worried about that too. "What if she falls on the stairs going down to the basement and I'm away and can't check on her that day? She'd be lying there for days. I worry about this shit; it keeps me up at night," Charles admitted.

"I'll look and see what I've got going on the next few weeks and plan to visit," I said. Charles's voice resonated with relief. I needed to see for myself what was going on.

I talked to Charles sporadically throughout the year—holidays, birthdays, that sort of thing. But he was calling me more often lately, each time more concerned about Mom. Today, I could tell by his agonized tone that he wanted my help.

Two weeks later, I was on a flight to Boston. Even though the temperatures were in the single digits, white puffy clouds blanketed the blue skyline. After the plane landed, I made my way through the terminal, hopped on the Hertz bus, retrieved my rental car, and began the one-and-a-half-hour drive to the Cape. Mom was expecting me.

Driving over the Sagamore Bridge with the Cape Cod Canal in clear view, I found myself thinking about my dad. This happened every time I crossed the bridge. I thought back to my happy childhood days spent on Cape Cod, and the way my dad always said proudly, "Here comes the bridge, kids!"

Twenty minutes later, I pulled onto the crushed seashell driveway of my mom's home—a two-bedroom Cape with weathered cedar shingles—and parked the car. The window boxes that were usually filled with fresh pink geraniums sat filled to the rims with snow. Icicles hung from the gutters. A swing hung low from a tree in the backyard rocking softly back and forth in the wind. Mom was waiting for me at the back door when I entered the house. When I hugged her, I felt jolted by how thin her five-foot-three-inch frame felt. Charles was right; she was frail. And I noticed that her hands were shaking. I wondered, *When was the last time I saw my mom in person? How did she lose so much weight?* While I set my luggage in the living room, I looked around. Nothing seemed out of the ordinary. But when I went to make a cup of tea in the kitchen, I found a mug in Mom's microwave filled with cold coffee.

"Mom, did you forget that you put coffee in the microwave?" I asked.

"I don't know, I probably did. I seem to be doing that a lot lately," she said.

"Mom, you look like you've lost weight. Are you eating all right?"

"Yeah, I think I am."

Her fridge was full, and there was plenty of food around. I calculated that it had been about eight months since I'd last seen her. It appeared that since then she'd lost about ten pounds. She seemed unsteady on her feet, and when I asked her what day of the week it was, she didn't know. I was worried and suggested to Charles and to my mom that we make a doctor's appointment for a checkup. Her doctor had an appointment available while I would be there, so we took it. After her appointment and all the lab tests were completed. Her doctor didn't seem concerned. Natural aging he said. "Just keep an eye on her weight."

Mom sat on one side of her round, light pine kitchen table, and I sat across from her. In the middle of the table sat a gold ceramic pot with a green ivy plant tucked inside. Sitting in white-and-pine matching chairs, we sipped on hot tea and caught up.

Over the course of thirty minutes, her cell phone rang three times. Mom didn't answer the first two times, but the third time, she sighed and said, "Oh, I'd better get this." I thought perhaps something serious had happened because someone was trying so desperately to reach her. When I found out it was my sister Marie, my irritation flared. Mom and I were trying to have a conversation, and the constant phone ringing was completely distracting. When she got off the phone, I asked, "Why was she calling you so much?"

"When she can't reach me, she freaks out and just keeps calling and calling until I finally answer."

"I thought something bad had happened," I said.

"Nope, she calls me all the time."

"How many times during the day does she call you?" I asked.

"Oh, I don't know—probably three or four, sometimes more."

"I don't understand why she needs to call you so much," I said.

"Sometimes it's a little annoying," Mom confessed, "but I'm all she has, Susan. Most of the time I really don't mind." For some reason I didn't believe her.

"Well, that would bug the shit out of me." I said as I picked up her phone to see the call history. While we had been out shopping the day before, Marie had called her six times. I had thought that was excessive, but then I learned that if Marie didn't talk to Mom every day, she'd worry excessively about our mother. Mom was getting older and frailer, so I understood.

In her passive tone, she said once again, "I really don't mind, Susan. I have nothing else to do." So, I let go of it.

I got up from my chair to make another cup of tea and thought about my upcoming visit with Marie and our other sister Joan. I was meeting them for lunch later that week, and I was determined to talk to Marie about her incessant calling.

I considered their dynamic. I knew Mom felt guilty for everything that had happened to Marie and for her role in not being a better protector, not standing up to my dad. When I got back to the table, I studied my mother. She suddenly looked all of her eighty-two years. Her new, brown-rimmed, tortoiseshell glasses hid her drooping eyelids. She had recently updated to a new style, and I told her she looked cool in them. "You're so hip, Mom," I said. When she smiled, she resembled a young child, one to whom compliments didn't come easy. I noticed the blue veins in her hand. *How did I miss that before*? As I watched her sip her tea, I could see that her hands shook.

Where had the time gone? It seemed like yesterday that I'd run home from school during second grade, finding my mother in the backyard talking with our neighbor, telling her that I thought I'd broken my finger in school and about the ether I had in the hospital that knocked me out and the surgery to realign the bone. I remembered my grandmother by my side. I thought about how I'd asked her to take me to J.M. Fields when I was in seventh grade to buy some pants because girls could finally wear pants in school, and I wanted to be one of the cool ones who wore them on the first day the rule had passed. I thought about when she told me that I should start wearing a bra and about when we had "the talk" about puberty and periods. And how special I felt when she bought me a beautiful silky white nightie and bathrobe set when I had my first child.

While we sat at the kitchen table, I'd been wanting to ask questions about Marie, and this seemed an opportune time. I pulled a journal from my bag to record anything important.

My mom looked at me bug-eyed and said, "Oh, wow, this looks serious."

"It's nothing, Mom. I have a few questions about Marie's illness. I just want to write down the answers, so I won't forget."

"Questions like what?"

But before I could get the first question out, she started in. "It was really hard to watch Marie deteriorate like that, ya know? It was so sad. I didn't know what to do. When something like that happens to your own daughter, you just don't know what to do."

I saw her shame and guilt rise to the surface, and the air was palpable with past pain. Emotions that she'd held in for so long showed in the distressed look on her face. Her eyes filled with tears, and her focus seemed to turn inward. She looked away from me briefly and stared into the distance. I was sure she was locked in her own world of memories. She sobbed and said, "I talk to Marie every day, Susan. I answer her phone calls because I feel so bad about what happened to her. Like I didn't do enough for her. I still find it hard to talk about. It was so hard getting her help back then. Your father fought me every inch of the way."

If my mother hadn't intervened to get Marie admitted when she was seventeen, my sister would most likely not have the quality of life she does today. She was originally diagnosed with schizophrenia, and then borderline personality disorder with schizophrenic tendencies which kept her in and out of psych hospitals for most of her twenties. A social worker checked in on her regularly, and she had routine medical checkups. She even held down a part-time job, cleaning offices at a bank after hours. She'd taken some classes at a local community college. She'd always shown an interest in the law, like my dad. I wondered, had her life turned out differently, whether she would have become a lawyer like him.

Over the years, she was hospitalized a few times, always after she stopped taking her medications. After each confinement, she'd be reintegrated into society and would have help finding a subsidized apartment and eventually another part-time job. It became a recurring pattern, and she relapsed every time. Since her last hospitalization about eight years earlier, she'd lived a relatively stable life.

When Marie relapsed, she became frightening. She became paranoid and spoke about conspiracies. She'd leave messages on my voicemail in a deep menacing tone that scared me. Her behavior reminded me of the day I'd locked myself in my parents' bedroom when she was talking in different languages. Although I felt bad for Marie and hated that she had to live with this awful illness, I kept my distance. I needed to for my own sanity.

Just the mention of Marie's illness sparked something in my mom. The emotions came out quick and raw. She'd most likely buried these feelings many years ago, where they'd remained stowed away until now. I urged Mom to set limits with Marie. "Just because you feel guilty about what happened to her, that doesn't mean that you have to tolerate her bugging you all the time," I said. "It's not your fault that she got sick—you can stop blaming yourself."

She remained quiet, her head down.

"I know it's an emotional topic, Mom, but we never talk about it. Even as a family back then, we never discussed what was happening to Marie or why. Or my dad's downfall and his alcoholism. We still don't talk about it. Nobody—none of us—knew what was happening. We had no clue why she was acting that way. Or why Dad suddenly lost it. It was really scary seeing her like that."

"Well, it was scary for me too," she said.

I wished that my mom would just acknowledge that Marie's illness, along with my dad's alcoholism, had had profound effects on the rest of the family. "I just wished that someone had told us what was going on," I said. "We needed to hear that at least that you were *aware* that something was happening to Marie and that you'd get to the bottom of it. I felt like we were just left to fend for ourselves."

Never acknowledging my comments about being left to scrape along, she asked, "Do you think it was the acid, Susan?"

"I don't know, Mom," I said, surprised to hear that she was still grappling, after all these years, with the reason for Marie's decline. "Maybe she was predisposed to schizophrenia, and it triggered something. All I know is that Marie was never the same after that, and I felt so bad that she never returned to her old self again."

"I never wanted to admit Marie to the hospital, but I had no choice," Mom said. She continued to ignore my comment about the effects of Marie's illness on the rest of the family, and my hope of opening a dialogue about that vanished. Her tunnel vision wasn't going away any time soon. And then, like a crossing guard signaling someone to stop, my mom raised her hand, palm facing me, and said, "That's enough, Susan. I can't talk about it anymore."

A minute later, she got up from her chair, walked over to the counter, and grabbed a tissue. That's when I noticed her nervous twitch. It was an involuntary movement—I don't think she even knew she did it. Every thirty seconds or so, her right shoulder shrugged up and then down. She did it mostly when she was standing or walking. I hadn't seen this movement in a long time. I'd remembered her doing it a lot when I was growing up, whenever she was stressed. That's how I knew I'd struck a nerve.

It was then I realized my mom had probably never spoken to anyone about any of this—her feelings, her shame, or the heartbreak she felt when her daughter was diagnosed with schizophrenia. She never got answers to her burning question of what caused Marie to get sick. I don't think she'll ever know. She's lived with this angst for decades. Now, as a mother myself, I thought of what it must have been like for her. I couldn't imagine what she'd gone through, and I suddenly felt a new tenderness toward her.

I wanted to say something that would take her pain away, but I really didn't know what to say. I got up from the chair, walked over to her, and hugged her. We cried together.

"I'm lucky I didn't go crazy, too," she said. "I'm a strong woman, and so are you, Susan." After a pause, she added, "Okay, can we not talk about the past anymore? What's past is past. I did the best I could."

I noticed that her arm was twitching again, but I said nothing about it.

As I wiped tears from my own eyes, I said to her, "I'm glad we talked about Marie, even for a little bit, Mom. It was cathartic for me just to talk about it out loud. I needed to. I hope it was somewhat cathartic for you too."

After my visit with Mom, I drove west for about two and half hours to Springfield to meet Marie and Joan for lunch. But first I wanted to make a visit to the Springfield YWCA—the one place that had helped me out when I'd first left Dave. I'd been in contact with the director, Mary Reardon, on the phone a few times but had never met her. For a number of years, I'd made donations to the YWCA at Christmas time, so we'd talked before, and she knew my story. At one point she suggested that if I was ever in the area, I should stop by and meet her. Today, I took her up on her offer. It had been almost thirty years to the day that I fled my home and found the safe haven of the Y. I was finally ready to find closure for that part of my life. I wanted to give thanks, to show them the face of a success story—of a woman who had fled an abusive situation and had gone on to live a life without violence and hate.

I pulled into the parking lot of the YWCA, parked my car, and made my way to the front door. My down-filled jacket kept me warm, and my sunglasses helped to fight the blinding sunlight that glistened against the recently fallen snow. That day, I entered the Springfield Y a very different woman than I'd been thirty years earlier. Although I'd never actually lived in the shelter, I'd spent many nights in a safe house as part of a YWCA support group. The meetings strengthened me and gave me hope of a life beyond abuse. Memories about the help I'd received from them flooded my consciousness, and I wanted to say a big thank you.

I entered the front door and was immediately greeted by a very friendly woman named Nancy. I told her why I was there. She said, "You have perfect timing. Mary was just getting ready to leave." Mary was getting ready to leave for her Cape Cod home for the weekend, and I was grateful that I'd caught her in time. I liked Mary immediately. We chatted in the entry lobby for a few moments, and I told her I'd just come from visiting my mom on Cape Cod. We talked about our favorite places on the Cape, something that people in love with that area do. We then ventured outside for a tour of the building.

"Wow, you have really come a long way," I said as I took in the newer brick-and-concrete buildings on the grounds. This was not the same building I'd gone to all those years ago. A tinge of pride hit me as I thought of my own journey and how much I'd changed in the past thirty years.

I could see Mary was proud, too, but there was a sadness in her reply. "Yeah, but not far enough," she said. "There is still so much work to do and not much has really happened in thirty years."

"What do you mean?" I asked.

"Well, the number of abused women has remained the same for so long now. No matter what we do, the statistics are just not changing. One in every eight women is living in an abusive situation. It was the same thirty years ago. Yes, there are a few more shelters, but the numbers aren't dropping."

We entered one of the buildings where the residents lived. If hope had an aroma, I smelled it now. The secure feeling of the building impressed me. *Wow, there was nothing available like this to me thirty years ago*, I thought. Gratitude and sadness engulfed me at the same time. My thoughts gravitated toward the women behind the closed doors and all of the women who had passed through here during the previous thirty years. I knew what they'd gone through, and I was immensely grateful that I'd made it out. I prayed for strength and hope for them, that they too would find happiness and be able to live a life free from harm. Free to become themselves.

A ten-minute drive away was the local Friendly's restaurant where I was to meet Marie and Joan. When I arrived, they were already sitting in a booth across from each other. After peeling off my winter gear, we hugged, and then I sat next to Marie. I didn't wait long before asking her about calling Mom so much. It was weighing on me, and I didn't have the patience to wait.

"I don't call her that much," she protested.

"I think you should try to call her less. She's getting older, and frankly it's annoying. Mom won't say anything to you, so I am."

Marie turned away from me and didn't answer. She just ignored me. "Just . . . please . . . try not to call her so much," I said as I picked up the menu.

More silence. Then she said, "I just worry about her, Susan. There's nothing the matter with that."

Even though I thought it was annoying, this was the pattern that my mom and Marie had developed over the years, and who was I to intervene now? I let it go.

After we ordered, Joan said, "Sue, I brought something I want you to see." She reached into her purse and pulled out a man's wallet. Worn around the edges, a chocolate-brown color. It was my father's.

I gasped and said, "Is that Dad's wallet?"

THE SIGHT OF his wallet sent me back into a daydream about the last time I'd seen that familiar, weathered piece of leather. It was in 1991 when he checked into the hospital six months before he died.

"Dad was admitted to the hospital today," my sister Sheila had said.

"For what?" I'd asked.

"I don't know," Sheila replied. I hung up the phone after she said she'd find out more and get back to me.

I had known that this day would come; I'd thought about it many times. I just hadn't thought it would be so soon. He was only sixty-two years old. I had always feared that one day his drinking would catch up to him. Was this that day? I was probably going to find out that he'd died in a terrible car accident or that he'd smashed his car into someone or something while driving plastered, or maybe even murdered an entire family. Maybe he was robbed and beaten up really bad—after all, he was hanging out in some pretty seedy joints.

My dad hated hospitals, so I knew it had to be bad. He didn't believe in doctors, and never went for yearly check-ups.

Sheila called me back later that day and told me Dad was having trouble breathing, so Joan had taken him to the hospital. He wasn't dead! And I was relieved that he hadn't killed anyone drunk driving.

The next day while working as a nurse on the fifth floor of the same hospital my dad was in, I went to see him during my lunch break. As I entered his room, his eyes widened. I'd heard a code blue, so I was extremely happy to see him sitting there in the bed. He seemed surprised but happy that I was there. He looked much older than I'd remembered. Worn out, tired.

At that point, it had been about fourteen years since my mom and dad had divorced. For most of that time, I'd kept my distance from him, and for the past few years we'd been completely estranged. That all changed that day in the hospital. For a brief moment, I was mad at myself for not seeing him for all those years. Instead of dwelling on that, I decided to try to reconnect with him.

He was dressed in a blue-and-white hospital johnny, loosely tied around his neck and slouched down in front exposing his gray chest hair. He looked to be in a state of disarray; the front of his hospital gown was stained with food, his hospital bootie socks were all twisted, the sheets were coming loose from the bed. I didn't like seeing my father like this. His skin was pale, his eyes were puffy, and he had a scruffy look about him. I was concerned about his shaking hands—I had to help him steady his coffee cup—and he repeated himself twice within five minutes. I had taken care of patients like this before, and I started to wonder if his doctor had prescribed any treatment for his alcoholism. I had taken care of a patient once who saw little green men running into the electrical socket in his hospital room. Surely, he had been going through withdrawal. I didn't want that to happen to my dad.

"How about I help you get cleaned up?" I asked him. "Would you like that?" I knew the nurses were busy because of the code blue, and bathing wasn't on the top of their list.

I went into the bathroom, filled the basin with warm water, and closed the curtain around his bed for privacy. I shaved his face, cleaned his feet and put lotion on them, and I even put powder under his arms like my mother used do for me when I was small. I had him sit in the recliner chair while I changed the sheets on his bed and neatly made it up. I fluffed his pillow. He got back into a nice clean bed. He smiled back with a tender expression.

"It's so good to see you, Susan," he said.

I teared up. It was at the moment that everything about my dad's drinking and what had transpired over the past fourteen years didn't matter anymore.

I said, "You too, Dad, it's been too long." He asked me about Sarah and Patrick and wanted to know if I had a picture of them that he could have. I told him that I would bring one by his room the next day. My heart felt warm. This would give me an excuse to check in on him.

I ran into the nurse in the hallway and learned that he would probably be able to be discharged in a few days. He was nearing the last dose of IV antibiotics for his respiratory infection and was getting better.

Back when my dad first left our house, detachment was my savior. I had to disassociate myself from seeing him—it was too painful for me. Now I no longer wanted to be detached. Beneath all the pain and sadness I'd felt about not seeing him all those years, I still felt a bond with him. I think it was probably because of all the years of therapy and support groups that I was now able to accept him and put judgment aside. I saw the dad I once knew, and I missed him.

For the first time in my adult life, I was nonjudgmental toward him. I felt only empathy. I knew he had a disease. Maybe it was the nurse in me that made me compassionate, and I was glad to have made it to this peaceful place, but I still kept my distance.

My dad was discharged less than a week later. He was better for a while, but then four months later, at the age of sixty-two, he passed away from a pulmonary embolism. He hadn't been feeling well and hadn't been able to eat for a few days. When he called Joan, she took him to the hospital, but he passed away in the emergency room. She had kept his wallet and its contents ever since.

"I've had this since Dad died," she told me, "but I haven't looked at it in a while."

Marie smiled at the image of our dad on his driver's license and said, "That's exactly how I remember him."

I held the license with both hands, caressed the plastic, and started crying as I looked at his picture. He was wearing his favorite orange cardigan, which made me smile through my tears.

As I looked through the rest of the wallet, I came upon something I wasn't expecting. Inside were the two school pictures of Sarah and Patrick that I'd given Dad that day in the hospital.

Sadness combined with pride and joy hit me hard—sadness from losing him twenty-three years earlier to alcoholism and thinking about what could have been. Pride and joy in knowing that my dad carried around my kids' pictures. I knew for sure that he still had his gentle soul intact. That, he never lost.

CHAPTER 20

NOVEMBER 2020

I am at my home in upstate New York sitting at my dark-brown-and-cream farm table in what I call my kitchen nook, looking out the six windows to the view of the grass-covered back yard where a stone wall leads to the patio. The white pines and the spruce are covered in snow. The other trees—the red oaks, the white birches, and the official New York State tree, the sugar maples—all sit void of leaves. Their naked branches take turns swaying wherever the wind takes them. I do love this time of year, not quite fall and not yet winter. My black lab mix, Max, sits on the floor under my feet. My other dog, Coco, an eight-month-old, Tri-colored Cavalier King Charles, is sound asleep on the sofa that abuts the nook. It's a cool, windy, snow flurry kind of day. Thirty-five degrees outside but feels more like twenty-five.

Ours was the first house built in this new six-lot cul-de-sac subdivision in Clifton Park, New York, when we moved in two years ago. Now I can hear the construction workers banging away with their hammers next door where there is a new house going up. House number three. To me, it is still peaceful and quiet. It feels like home. Everything I've been through has led me here. I am grateful for the peacefulness that I never knew growing up but live with now. I now have peace, safety, and love.

What I didn't see coming was that just one year after the conversation during which my brother would express so much worry about my mother, I would move from St. Louis to upstate New York and would move my mother in with us. Nor had I guessed that soon after, she'd be diagnosed with Alzheimer's disease. Nor would I have thought that within two years, she wouldn't be able to be left by herself or that she wouldn't know what day or year it was. I didn't anticipate that she'd have to rely on others to care for her. And I couldn't have guessed that she'd forget my birthday.

Like the movie *Ground Hog Day*, I'd find out that each day with my mom was a new day but with the same conversations. Each day different but the same. Memories from the previous day never stuck around.

Three years earlier, I would never have imagined that my mom would sit at my kitchen counter coloring in an adult coloring book with colored pencils for hours. And when she wasn't doing that, she'd work on a puzzle. I would come to mourn the loss of my mother as I had known her. But in the disappearing of the old mom came a new mom with a lot of loving gestures and "I love yous." I'd become grateful for that.

My mom would eventually need my brother and me to speak for her when she no longer could.

I didn't yet know that I would spend days crying about the lack of communication in my family and indecision over what to do about mom and where she should live. A rift would form among my siblings when Mom started to live in a memory care unit close to me.

During this three-year period—because of the craziness of my family dynamics and the exhaustion in navigating the rolling waves of turmoil after years of calm—I would again begin to feel like that sensitive child I had been. The dynamics among my six siblings remain the same as they were in childhood. Because I was the only one addressing our mother's needs and wanting to be proactive in dealing with it, the majority of them viewed me as bossy—a know it all.

After a two-year-long good-bye, my mother succumbed to

Alzheimer's disease in August of 2020, during the COVID-19 pandemic.

I wish I could say that we are a tight family unit and that we all get along pretty well, that we respect each other, listen to each other without judgment and support one another—no matter what. Sadly, I cannot. Although I remain close to a few of my siblings, the closeness, the camaraderie of a tight original family unit never existed for me and still doesn't. I've wondered over the years if that's because we all went into self-protection mode at a young age and whether some of us might still be in that mode.

I have long accepted my past and better understand the choices I've made along my life's journey. The excursion of revisiting my past also led me to view my parents through an adult lens, which has offered me a better understanding of them. I came away able to forgive myself and to believe that my parents did the best they could with the tools they had. I know that they loved me and my siblings; that I never questioned. But I needed a lot of time to understand and accept the reasons they couldn't show us love. Coming to grips with all that has allowed me to move forward.

That shy girl inside of me saw the world in a different way, and I wanted her voice to be heard and shared. Her sensitivity is still alive and well in me.

We live in a world of constant searching, the longing to feel loved, to be loved and to give love. I've come to believe that the one thing in life that really matters is love.

Like a lotus flower, we all have the ability to rise from muddy waters, to bloom out of the darkness and radiate into the world.

THE END

EPILOGUE

To be loved
Is to know happiness and contentment
To give love is to know
The joy of sharing oneself . . .
For it is through
the miracle of love
That we discover
the fullness of life.

—ROBIN ST. JOHN

I remain close to my sister Marie. We talk often. She lives on her own in an apartment in Massachusetts and is doing well. She has a cat, goes for daily walks, and is very proud of the fact that she quit smoking years ago. As long as she continues to take her prescribed medication, she remains stable. The other day she told me, "I don't hear voices anymore."

My twin sister, Sheila stayed married to Jesse for a brief period, then divorced. She eventually remarried and had two more children. She is alive and well living in Massachusetts.

Joan did not marry Jamie and lived with my mom until her daughter was about ten years old. She married and went on to have three more children. She is alive and well and also living in Massachusetts.

My only brother Charles has always held a special place in my heart. He is the only one that gets my sense of humor. He has two children is alive and well and lives in Cape Cod Massachusetts. He is engaged to be married.

The younger set of twins: Mary is married and has four grown children. She is alive and well living in Massachusetts. We remain close, and once a year we plan a sister trip away together. She lives south of Boston, Massachusetts.

Margaret is married and has two grown children. She is alive and well and lives east of Boston, Massachusetts.

Sarah is now in her late thirties, happily married with two gorgeous children. They live in Massachusetts.

My son Patrick is also in his late thirties, happily married and the father of two beautiful children. He and his sister live near each other in Massachusetts and maintain contact with their father.

Samantha is single, in her late twenties and living in upstate New York.

ACKNOWLEDGMENTS

To my children: being your mom is my most precious gift in life. Your love saved me. You will forever be a part of me.

To my grandchildren: may you never know suffering and pain, and may you always rise above your challenges. May you always hold the innocence that I see in you today. Your love is indescribable and makes me want to live forever.

To my Mom: I am thankful for your strength when it was needed, for your growth when it was right for you, and for your unspoken love. I miss you. Dad, thank you for loving me.

I will be forever grateful to the Springfield YWCA who saved my life, from Brenda who ushered me into a safe world to the legal advocate who helped me in court to the many women who chaired a support group. You were all part of my journey, and no matter how lovely and exciting my life may become I will never forget how it felt to be sad and frightened. You gave me hope and strength.

To Patrick Ward, my attorney from Springfield, Massachusetts: thanks for having my back and for your ultimate friendship. May you rest in peace.

Katie and Steve: thank you for caring so much. Your support, love, and strength got me through one of the most difficult times in my young adult life. I will be forever grateful to you both for opening your house to me when I had nowhere else to go.

To all of my friends and family who sent me get well wishes during my cancer treatments: your words held me together. I want to thank especially my cousin Jill. You never forgot about me. When the rest of the well-wishes dried up, I always found an uplifting card in my mailbox from you. You don't know how much that meant to me.

My Yale New Haven friends, especially Ellen: thanks for being there when I really needed someone. I miss you tremendously.

To Beez and Ruth, my friends in St. Louis who supported me during the start of my memoir: your never-ending friendship helped me get through many tough days as I delved into buried memories.

To Scott, my muse: thanks for making my workout days never boring and for your friendship and conversations. I miss you and them.

To Jean my therapist in St. Louis who came to me when I needed someone to help me process what was going on in my heart and head: I am thankful that you introduced me to the process of EMDR.

To my first writing teachers, Linda Joy Myers, Judy Mandel, and Jerry Waxler: thank you for introducing me to the exciting world of memoir writing. You were all so encouraging. I never knew how much my life would change when I signed up for your memoir writing class on the Connecticut shore so many years ago. Your passion for the craft of memoir writing has remained with me ever since. Also, thank you Judy for your first editing and for telling me to "keep writing."

To Katherine Mayfield and Jennifer Craven: because of your honest editing and feedback, I kept writing.

To Brooke Warner of She Writes Press: your professional expertise and coaching was something I looked forward to every week. Thank you to you and your entire team for helping me make this memoir what I envisioned it to be.

To Crystal Patriarche and the team at BookSparks: thank you for your vision and professional expertise.

A very special heartfelt thank you to Cindy my psychotherapist, who has worked with me for over thirty years and has somehow helped me keep my sanity intact. You have walked through the pains of my past with me. Digging through the layers of my psyche was debilitating, but with your guidance I arrived on the other side of pain and suffering. I would not be the person I am today if it weren't for you.

To Charles: I look forward to growing old with you on the Cape. To my sister and BFF, Mary: I never want to envision my life without you. Your friendship, unconditional love, and support mean the world to me.

Most of all I want to thank my husband Bruce: you are the true love of my life. I am sincerely blessed that I found someone I can share my life's journey with and be my true self with. You have loved me through the good, the bad, and the ugly. Your love and support are my lifelines to normalcy.

ABOUT THE AUTHOR

Credit: Emily Elisabeth Photography

SUSAN FRANCES MORRIS was raised in Springfield, Massachusetts, the second oldest of seven siblings that included two sets of twins. She was a practicing nurse from 1989 to 2011, primarily in Women's Health. The highlight of her career was the time she spent at Yale New Haven Hospital in New Haven, Connecticut, working in nursing management alongside international experts in the field of women's health.

Her passions are spending time in nature, walking or bike riding, practicing yoga, traveling, practicing photography, and designing jewelry. She has three grown children and four grand-children. She lives with her husband and two dogs in Clifton Park, New York.

SELECTED TITLES FROM SHE WRITES PRESS

She Writes Press is an independent publishing company
founded to serve women writers everywhere.
Visit us at www.shewritespress.com.

Patchwork: A Memoir of Love and Loss by Mary Jo Doig. $16.95, 978-1-63152-449-3. Part mystery and part inspirational memoir, Patchwork chronicles the riveting healing journey of one woman who, following the death of a relative, has a flashback that opens a dark passageway back to her childhood and the horrific secrets that have long been buried deep inside her psyche.

The First Signs of April: A Memoir by Mary-Elizabeth Briscoe. $16.95, 978-1631522987. Briscoe explores the destructive patterns of unresolved grief and the importance of connection for true healing to occur in this inspirational memoir, which weaves through time to explore grief reactions to two very different losses: suicide and cancer.

Raising Myself: A Memoir of Neglect, Shame, and Growing Up Too Soon by Beverly Engel. $16.95, 978-1-63152-367-0. A powerfully inspiring and unflinchingly honest story of how best-selling author and abuse recovery expert Beverly Engel made her way in the world—in spite of her mother's neglect and constant criticism, undergoing sexual abuse at nine, and being raped at twelve.

Say It Out Loud: Revealing and Healing the Scars of Sexual Abuse by Roberta Dolan. $16.95, 978-1-938314-99-5. An in-depth guide to healing the wounds caused by sexual abuse, written by a survivor who's lived the process firsthand.

Baffled by Love: Stories of the Lasting Impact of Childhood Trauma Inflicted by Loved Ones by Laurie Kahn. $16.95, 978-1631522260. For three decades, Laurie Kahn has treated clients who were abused as children—people who were injured by someone who professed to love them. Here, she shares stories from her own rocky childhood along with those of her clients, weaving a textured tale of the all-too-human search for the "good kind of love."